John Ashbrook

The Pocket Essential

TERRY GILLIAM

www.pocketessentials.com

First published in Great Britain 2000 by Pocket Essentials, 18 Coleswood Road, Harpenden, Herts, AL5 1EQ

Distributed in the USA by Trafalgar Square Publishing,P.O. Box 257, Howe Hill Road, North Pomfret, Vermont 05053

A CIP catalogue record for this book is
available from the British Library.

ISBN 1-903047-14-5

9 8 7 6 5 4 3 2 1

Book typeset by Nikita
Printed and bound by Cox & Wyman

"Because I dislike being quoted, I find I lie almost constantly when talking about my work."
- *Gilliam quoted by Kim 'Howard' Johnson in Starlog #92*

"I have learned from experience that a modicum of snuff can be most efficacious!"
- *Baron Munchausen, upon being swallowed by a great fish*

Dedicated to Maureen and Andy Ashbrook,
for keeping it unreal.

Acknowledgements

This book was brought to you by REM, Skunk Anansie, The Shamen, Led Zeppelin, David Bowie, Andy Marsh, Mike Old-field, Pearl Jam, Tea, Mark and Lard, Virgin Cola, lashings of Hawkwind and a lone male voice, with the remnants of an American accent, way off in the distance.

Man of the match was the noble Phil Stubbs, master of Dreams and Gilliam's internet biographer. Richard Luck and David Morgan carried the magic sponge. Sympathetic noises were made by the ingenious Steve Holland, for whom the impossible isn't; and the ubiquitous Ellen Cheshire, for whom the possible isn't, if it involves computers.

My love to you all...in a very real and legally-binding sense.

Contents

Introduction: Intimations Of Immortality

"Terry Gilliam: He Giggled In Awe."
- obituary found on a gravestone, somewhere in the 21st century.

Do you believe in synchronicity? No, it's not just a Police album – it is as my dictionary has it: 'A parallel or synchronous occurrence.' The reason I ask, is because the finest film fantasists of the modern era, The Brothers Coen and Terry Gilliam, were all born in the shadow of Minneapolis, Minnesota. What are the chances of that? There must be something in the water.

Terrence Vance Gilliam was born there on November 22 1940, the first-born son of Beatrice Gilliam (née Vance) and James Hall. As they lived on the outskirts of the big city, in a town called Medicine Lake, he spent his infant years playing in the local swamp and absorbing the rural atmosphere.

By the early 50s the family, having clearly decided it was just too damn chilly up north, relocated to the new town of Panorama City in the San Fernando Valley. That's the place on the *other* side of the Hollywood sign. It seems even Gilliam's parents had an eye for the ironic.

It was in California, living near all those movie studios, that Gilliam developed a taste for cinema popcorn. One of his earliest film memories would have a decisive influence on his fledgling imagination and form a significant inspiration for the film *Time Bandits*: "The movie that got me as a kid, gave me nightmares for years, was *The Thief Of Bagdad* (1940)...They were good nightmares, filled with wondrous, inventive things. There's something about finding a bottle with a genie in it who can make anything happen." [1]

Gilliam swept into Occidental College in LA as a Physics major. After this, he tried Art, then dipped his toe in Political Science. All the while, what he was really doing was editing *Fang*, a college magazine modelled after the satirical magazines of Harvey Kurtzman: *Mad* and *Help!*

After concentrating on his studies just long enough to graduate in 1962, Gilliam made his way to New York and waltzed into the *Help!* offices. He had sent issues of *Fang* to Kurtzman and received encouraging responses, so decided to cash them in. Showing timing a childless Catholic would be proud of, he arrived just as Assistant Editor Charles Alverson was leaving, so found himself installed behind Alverson's desk, enjoying his first real job, with the ink hardly dry on his College Diploma.

Among many other things, Gilliam was put in charge of the 'fumetti' section of the magazine. This was an idea Kurtzman had pinched from the Italians – presenting comic strip stories with photos instead of drawings. One of the out-of-work actors Gilliam found himself photographing was an Englishman called John Cleese, who was in New York as part of a Cambridge Footlights tour.

After three years in New York, *Help!* gasped its last. Back in LA, Gilliam made ends meet as a cartoonist, whilst also working as a photographer for his English journalist girlfriend, Glenys Roberts. He dallied briefly with legitimacy as a Copywriter and Art Director for an advertising firm then, in 1967, when Roberts expressed a desire to return to England, he gladly tagged along. We haven't been able to get rid of him since.

Whilst continuing with the cartooning for *The Sunday Times*, among others, Gilliam decided that he was bored with magazines. The only non-magazine person he knew in London was Cleese, who was by this time nicely installed in the BBC, working on *The Frost Report*. Gilliam asked Cleese to put him in touch with any TV producers. Cleese directed him to Humphrey Barclay, who was in charge of the children's show *Do Not Adjust Your Set*. Gilliam bombarded Barclay with cartoons, and also with his first attempts at written sketches. Barclay bought some, and Gilliam was in. The actors on the show included Michael Palin, Terry Jones, and Eric Idle who, being legendarily gregarious, made friends with the strange long-haired American, even when the others wouldn't.

Barclay moved over to London Weekend Television and set up the comedy show *We Have Ways Of Making You Laugh*. He took Gilliam and Idle with him. Meanwhile, Palin, Jones, Cleese and Graham Chapman had all been writing for Marty Feldman's first solo show *Marty*, whilst Gilliam had been asked to animate some of his cartoons for the show.

Inspired by the 50s political animations of Stan Vanderbeek, who used photo collages, and chastened by the absence of time or money, Gilliam developed a very simple, very quick method of moving about cut-outs. He would interweave images from photos and paintings with his own cartoons, using his new toy – the airbrush.

Barry Took was the BBC's Head Of Comedy at that time, and had extended to Cleese (the relative star of the group) an offer to develop any show he liked. He liked the idea of working with his group of friends on a stream-of-consciousness show, heavily influenced by Spike Milligan's *Q5*, which would run one sketch into another without need of a punchline (always the most difficult part of comedy writing) and would link some sketches together with surreal animations.

That'll be *Monty Python's Flying Circus* then!

In 1974, Gilliam married one of the *Python* make-up girls, Maggie Weston, who, in between spawning mini-Gilliams, continued to work as make-up artist on her husband's early films. To ensure that the madness continues, they have three children: Amy Rainbow (born in 1977), Holly du Bois (born in 1980) and Harry Thunder (born in 1988).

Of his working practice on *Python*, Gilliam says: "...when the others got really stuck, they'd say 'Gilliam takes over from here and takes us to there.' So I was pleased to be working within the parameters of A to B, even if they were totally unconnected. That freed me because I totally seize up when I have the possibility of total freedom – the choices become infinite and I go round in circles not knowing where to begin." [2]

He began by studying dusty old painters no one else had heard of. Firstly he would take inspiration *from* the work of these masters, then he would take the scissors *to* them. The first and, purely by dint of its repetition, the most obvious of these incorporations was from a painting hanging in London's National Gallery. It was *An Allegory (Venus, Cupid, Time and Folly)* (1540-45) by the Florentine Mannerist Agnolo Bronzino, whose religious and allegorical paintings shine with a technical virtuosity and a seductive empathy for the glory of naked human flesh, which few have equalled before or since. He was also a dab hand at painting feet, and Gilliam needed a foot, a big one, to finish off the title sequence.

Unsurprisingly, given the visual and intellectual complexity of his films, Gilliam's animations are knee-deep in meaning and metaphor: "A lot of the cartoons I did for *Python* were very disturbing. There's a lot of anger, anarchy and nihilism along with the bright colours and silly pictures...There's the odd dodo out there who just likes colour and noise, and if people want to look at the surface, it's an entertaining surface, but if they want to look deeper there are other things going on." [3]

Palin said of Gilliam's work: "It's the most wild and exciting part of Python, I think, the Gilliam edge. If Python was made up of six Gilliams, there would be this total explosion of creativity and bits of Pythons spattered all over the walls." [4]

If an exhaustive, in-depth analysis of Gilliam's *Python* work exists, I haven't found it. Such a book certainly deserves to be written, but this isn't it. In fact, we shall bid a fond adieu to *Monty Python*'s original tele-visual manifestation at this point and move on, since the movies are our primary concern.

Since venturing out from the protective shadow of the Monty Python team, in the mid-70s, Gilliam has gone on to produce a unique body of filmic work. He has been far more consistently successful at this than any of his alumni yet, each time he dons the director's jodhpurs and beret, he seems to find himself fighting against the legions of corporate bureaucracy. Despite the fact that his films have made money, the studios don't trust him. Despite that fact that some of the biggest, baldest movie stars ever to have trodden the Hollywood Hills are prepared to undergo immense humiliation just to appear in his films, the studios don't trust him. Despite the fact that he has been afforded the as-yet rare privilege of having a *Pocket Essential* written about him whilst he's still alive enough to sue, you can bet that the studios still won't trust him.

Which is, I suppose, only fair; since he doesn't trust them either.

I don't want to spend too much of the precious space I have here, dwelling on the Herculean efforts Gilliam has made to get his films out there, every cut and thrust of which is very well documented elsewhere: the books *The Battle Of Brazil* by Jack Mathews and *Losing The Light* by Andrew Yule, being the most obvious examples.

Similarly, I don't want to concentrate too much on Gilliam's own rec-ollections of the film-making process. Again, this ground has been thor-oughly raked over in *Gilliam On Gilliam* by Ian Christie, then trampled all over again by *Dark Knights And Holy Fools* by Bob McCabe. These are both excellent volumes, my only proviso being that, since there are only so many ways Gilliam can tell the same anecdotes and still make them funny, the books are somewhat repetitive repetitive. Both of the above tomes were published within a year of the volume you now clasp in your timorous grasp. That's the problem with Gilliam books, you wait 10 years, then three of 'em come along at once.

So, if I'm not going to be concentrating on Gilliam himself, what am I going to be spending 96 pages doing? I'm going to be looking at the films themselves. Certainly, they will reveal something of the personal-ity of their maker, since they are all very personal statements, and they all have many concerns and motifs in common. All that will develop naturally as we become more familiar with the films.

When discussing the first public screening of his first solo feature, *Jabberwocky*, Gilliam laments: "[the audience] didn't know what to make of these beautiful images alongside the crass humour. Then I got up and charmed them, and they all started liking the movie because they liked me. This always makes me crazy because I want the movies to be judged in their own right." [5]

Well, now is their chance.

I will now attempt to outline some of the major themes I see in Gilliam's films. In order to do this, I will occasionally be forced to employ some strong words, such as 'Freudian,' 'repression' and 'vicious maneating fluffy bunny.' You may wish to cut these words out with a pair of rounded scissors, before allowing small children to play with this book. After all, we don't want to give them ideas!

On the audio commentary of the Criterion DVD of *Time Bandits*, David Warner quotes Orson Welles, in calling film "the ribbon of dreams," then generously adds that: "Terry is one of the wonderful and few directors who can put his dreams and nightmares actually onto celluloid." [6]

Indeed, I would say that dream imagery is more prevalent in Gilliam's work than in that of anyone else working in live-action film today, with the possible exception of David Lynch. As any tinpot amateur psychologist can tell you, dreams are our way of dealing with issues that confuse or trouble us, our way of exploring ideas and concepts which maybe we can't go near in the real world.

Fiction, if it serves any purpose at all, similarly allows us to explore modes of expression which our circumstance or confidence prevents. David Fincher's satire *Fight Club* (1999), demonstrated what a detrimental effect lack of sleep, and therefore lack of dreaming, can have on the human psyche. If we can't deal with these demons in fantasy, we may find ourselves facing them for real.

There is a notion among critics that Gilliam's six main films (conveniently ignoring *Jabberwocky*) fall into two thematically-linked trilogies. This theory is so artificially neat, one is desperate for him to make a seventh 'dream' film, just to spoil it. However, it is generally true that, in *Time Bandits*, *Brazil* and *The Adventures Of Baron Munchausen*, the fantasies are a positive force in the lives of the dreamers, offering them

11

compensations for the shortcomings of the real world. In the later films, *The Fisher King*, *12 Monkeys* and *Fear And Loathing In Las Vegas*, the fantasies are far more problematic, often even damaging the dreamer. Let's look at some of the theories which surround dreams.

Fantasy derives from our dreams' capacity to suspend disbelief and explore areas which would feel a little too extreme if we had to face them awake. These sleep experiences spill over into our waking life when, for example, we are re-experiencing them through watching a film or TV show. Robin Wood, in the introduction to his book *The American Nightmare* states: "The old tendency to dismiss the Hollywood cinema as escapist always defined escape merely negatively as escape *from*, but escape must logically also be escape *to*." [7]

This is a fair assessment of the general purpose of fantasy, withdrawing from a reality where you can't have what you want and need, to a made-up world where you can.

To an extent, it is true that the willingness to succumb to fantasy denotes an unhappiness with reality. Stands to reason. However, the Freudians take this argument further: "According to Freudian theory, the infant at birth is an undifferentiated mass of needs...its hunger is satisfied by its mother...but its mother often goes away, causing a sense of loss. In fantasy, the child starts to wish for power over the mother. It is loss that leads to the development of fantasy. But the fantasy is impossible, not least because the mother is 'owned' by the father. So, hand in hand with fantasy comes repression." [8]

Unfortunately, the desires expressed in fantasy are inevitably transgressive, illegal and probably painful, otherwise we wouldn't have a problem with trying them out for real. The usual one quoted is the Oedipal incest wish – ' I want to have sex with mummy, so must kill daddy first' - Y'know, that kind of thing. This then, is why we must explore these desires, if we have them (and Freudians would say that we do, yes, even you), in the auditorium of our imagination.

However, orthodox religions being the manipulative and controlling institutions they are, Western society has developed around a strict moral framework, which frowns upon liberation in any form, even liberation of mind (at least among the working classes), and we are therefore taught from a very early age that such thoughts are taboo. We quickly learn to look upon our own perfectly natural thought processes as something of which we should be ashamed. Therefore, because we so desperately need to conform and feel normal, the desire is frequently repressed, buried, ignored.

"Freud always insisted on the 'indestructibility of the contents of the unconscious.' Repressed material not only escapes destruction, it also has a permanent tendency to re-emerge into consciousness...by more or less devious routes." [9]

Robin Wood believes that this re-emergence of repressed desire is fundamental to the creation of monsters both within the imagination and on the cinema screen. So, unless you want a masked, hatchet-wielding, undead psychopath to lop off your precious extremities, you'd better have sex as frequently and as imaginatively as possible.

At least, I think that's what Wood is saying. I've got a lot of explaining to do, if not. Either way, Gilliam's films interrogate such notions, often by playing with them. I'll be bringing these ideas to bear on his films, where appropriate, and seeing how they stand up.

Grotesquerie is, likewise, a representation of the ways we attempt to deal with transgressive desires and the resulting anxiety. But the Grotesque image is more personally and precisely aimed at exploring the weaknesses of our too, too sullied flesh.

One of the major motifs of The Grotesque, is the depiction of Death, not as an amorphous abstract but as a bloke with a scythe, as in *Munchausen*, *Monty Python's Meaning Of Life* and innumerable Terry Pratchett books. Furthermore, Grotesquerie delights in investigating all the dark fleshy, functional parts of the human body which are commonly not discussed in polite society:

"Eating, drinking, defecating and other eliminating, as well as copulation, pregnancy, dismemberment, swallowing up by another body...the artistic logic of the grotesque image ignores the closed, smooth and impenetrable surface of the body and retains only its excrescences and orifices...Mountains and abysses, such is the relief of the grotesque body." [10]

Grotesquerie is a form of aversion therapy, rubbing our noses in all the facts of life our anxieties would have us forget. The British are traditionally so reserved, so repressed, that we are incapable of being honest about something as simple as a fart. That is why, in Britain at least, farting has comedic value – through understanding, recognition and, of course, relief.

Dominant culture very often employs our fear of embarrassment, our fear of our own fleshy functions, to repress us. This, combined with our fear of our own unrealised desires, makes us pretty screwed up, emotionally.

The only hope, therefore, for those of us unable to unleash our libidos and proudly fart and shag our way to emotional stability, is to point and laugh and vicariously burn the effigies of those things which, were they real, would horrify and dominate us. Fantasy fiction, by presenting us with these horrors in a safe, controllable way, helps us deal with the demons which lurk in our own primordial minds. So, producing scatological comedy is actually a public service!

Jabberwocky introduces this with its jousting contest – going from the blood and guts of the losing competitors spraying the royal box, to the delightfully childish hide-and-seek game of the survivors.

This is just the Python sketch *Sam Peckinpah's Salad Days* writ large, but it does serve to introduce the fine line which separates horror from humour. In a horror movie, this much bloodletting would be designed to get teenage girls to cling to their boyfriends for protection. In *Jabberwocky*, the grue is used in the way that politically correct comics employ offensive jokes – to stretch and interrogate perceptions of good and bad taste.

Society paints an emulsion of respectability and euphemism over the perfectly normal and natural, and Gilliam clearly insists on peeling back that paint to expose the embarrassments beneath. In *Time Bandits*, Kevin's ultra-conservative parents have wrapped their house in a sheen of plastic to keep it hygienic and safe. In *Brazil*, when Spoor and Dowser are systematically destroying Sam Lowry's apartment, they wear clear sealed-plastic suits, which will become their graves. Many movies later, Bruce Willis has to wrap himself in several layers of transparent plastic before venturing out into the supposedly unclean world. He, like Kevin in *Time Bandits*, needs to get out into the world in order to grow, earn some experiences and get some dirt under his fingernails.

Of course, there is much more to Grotesquerie than just shitting and farting. There's the whole wide world of aggressive transgression. Much fantasy fiction, from the Marquis de Sade and the Gothics onwards, transgresses (often violently) social taboos through the literal depiction of the imaginary. Another way to rub taboos up the wrong way, is through deliberate inversion or juxtaposition. For example: "...the original grotesque paintings described by Vitruvius and imitated by Renaissance painters [feature] the interweaving of plant, animal, human and architectural forms, so that the stone pedestal would become the torso of a human figure with curling plants for arms and an animal's head." [11]

In *Time Bandits*, Evil mulls over what to turn the Bandit, Og into: "Half donkey, half warthog, half oyster, half carrot?" This is a fair representation of Gilliam's working practice. With his animations, he would literally paste together patently inappropriate images cut from magazines and photographs. In his films, he is ceaselessly collaborationist, cheerfully 'cutting and pasting' the suggestions of his co-workers to supplement his own ideas.

Of course, all such grotesque creations echo the Chimera of Greek mythology - a fire-breathing animal with the head of a lion, the body of a goat and the tail of a serpent. Closely allied to this Chimeric instinct, is The Grotesque's penchant for tearing bodies asunder. The paintings of Hieronymus Bosch had a profound effect on Gilliam, which is particularly clear in his earlier films, which are packed with disturbing Chimeric creatures, as well as far more than their fair share of naked bodies being castrated, beheaded, eviscerated or eaten. Bosch was creating literal depictions of the fear that ran through his society: fear of God, fear of the plague, fear of authority, fear of revolution.

Throughout Gilliam's films, you will find many examples of heads being removed. These images contribute to Gilliam's grotesque interest in dismembering, but also come from the fantasy motif of using decapitation images as symbolic of our anxiety over castration. It's all that Freud stuff again!

Other restrictions that the fantastic and grotesque happily ignore, are the rules of space and time. So it is that Baron Munchausen can float to the moon in a balloon, whilst getting younger the more his self-confidence builds, and *Time Bandits* and *12 Monkeys* feature characters who zip backwards and forwards through time and space.

The fantastic and the grotesque are two important aspects of Gilliam's work which I will explore in detail. Other common motifs you will notice include his eye for elaborate, Heath Robinson-esque machinery. This originates from the Summer of 1960, when Gilliam spent three months working on the line of the Chevrolet assembly plant, feeling like a small and unimportant cog in a huge, soulless machine. This fascination/obsession can be seen in his 1971 title-sequence animation for *The Marty Feldman Comedy Machine* (reprinted almost frame-by-frame in his book *Animations Of Mortality*).

Whilst such user-surly machines are an obvious ingredient of *Brazil* and *Munchausen*, they can also be found in *Jabberwocky*'s armour-garage, in Evil's Fortress in Time Bandits, and remain prevalent in the underground warrens of *12 Monkeys*. This fascination even continued through to his inspirational involvement with the *Devious Devices* exhibition which toured Britain in early 1998.

There are many other ideas repeated throughout the films, most of which I simply won't be able to explore since the list is too long. I will concentrate on my favourites. However, I reserve the right to broach a few of these alternative subjects as and when I see fit. For example, the struggle of the individual over the anonymous machinations of bureaucracy which can be seen in *Brazil* and *The Crimson Permanent Assurance*, and in the crushing of the skilled craftsmen by the march of progress in *Jabberwocky*, and by the dwarves' rebellion against The Supreme Being in *Time Bandits*.

As Keith Hamel notes on the *Dreams* website, this theme is also demonstrated in Gilliam's constant contrasting of scale. Since his sympathy lies with the individual, the little man, he delights in making his heroes as small and as vulnerable as possible, whilst the societies from which they must escape are intimidatingly vast. Therefore, it would have to be a group of dwarves which rebel against the great bureaucracy in the sky. The fall of the labyrinthine Ministry of Information begins in an office too small to fit in a whole desk. "Taking this motif further, Gilliam tends to use very small and simple things to disrupt, and sometimes even destroy, the large and complex structures of modernity...a virus (microscopic in nature) almost destroys the human race (and everything else) in *12 Monkeys*." [12]

Allied with this, is Gilliam's mistrust of unregulated progress. *Time Bandits* insists unambiguously that technology encourages the ambitions of Evil, whilst *Munchausen* is a rounding critique of the whole concept of the Age of Reason and the death of imagination. Similarly, *The Fisher King* demonstrates that, even at an advanced stage in that Age of Reason, rationality and medical science can fail where simple faith succeeds.

Hamel also notes Gilliam's penchant for circular narratives, for ending his films roughly where they began – the zoom in to the map to begin *Time Bandits*, the zoom out to end it. The close-up of young Cole's eyes which book-ends *12 Monkeys*. The way the Baron's adventures begin and end in the theatre. How the American version of *Brazil* begins and ends with images of billowing clouds. As he puts it: "Unlike most films, which unfold from beginning to end, Gilliam's films seem to move in the opposite direction. After seeing the ending, the audience almost always rethinks the beginning." [13]

One final motif which I deeply regret having to leave out, is the tightly-woven pattern of references which thread through the material of all Gilliam's films. From simple parody, to pastiche to deeply respectful homage, Gilliam evokes classical painters, great film-makers, significant movie moments and even, most mischievously, his own previous films.

All of these details pile onto the storylines, burying the meanings and motives in layers of strata which require the viewer to indulge in a mental archaeological dig if they are to unearth just what the film is really about. This is rarely as obvious as it may, at first glance, appear.

Of course, until quite recently, Gilliam himself resisted the claims to intellectual depth made for his films. At the time of *Jabberwocky*'s release, he said: "Some people are already taking it seriously, and seeing in the picture socio-economic-religious pretensions. Could it be that the reviews, particularly in France, might be funnier than the film?" [14]

This reticence is not at all surprising, since the fantastic and grotesque are built upon a healthy disregard for the serious and authoritative. Still, since this book is neither serious nor authoritative, I guess that means I'm safe from Gilliam's derision!

Quotes:
1: Gilliam quoted in Jack Mathews, *Earth To Gilliam*, *American Film*, March 1989, p34
2: Gilliam quoted in Ian Christie, *Gilliam On Gilliam*, p43
3: Gilliam quoted in Leslie Bennetts, *How Terry Gilliam Found A Happy Ending For Brazil*, *New York Times*, January 19 1986, Section 2, p15
4: Palin quoted in Lewis Grossberger, *Monty Python*, *People*, August 2 1982, p46
5: Gilliam quoted in Ian Christie, *Gilliam On Gilliam*, p76
6: David Warner quoted on the Criterion Collection edition of *Time Bandits*
7: Robin Wood, *The American Nightmare*, p13
8: Martin Barker, *Comics: Ideology, Power And The Critics*, pp213-14
9: J P Laplanche & J P Pontalis, *Language of Psychoanalysis*, p313
10: Bakhtin quoted in ibid p42

11: Philip Thomson quoted in John O Thompson, *Monty Python's Complete And Utter Theory Of The Grotesque*, p14
12: Keith Hamel, *Dreams: Gilliam Motifs*, July 28 1997
13: ibid
14: Gilliam quoted in John O Thompson, *Monty Python's Complete And Utter Theory Of The Grotesque*, p19

Part One: Bronzino's Foot

Monty Python And The Holy Grail (1974)

"Dennis, there's some lovely filth down here."

Cast: Chapman (King Arthur), Cleese (Sir Launcelot, Black Knight, Tim The Enchanter, French Soldier), Idle (Sir Robin, Concord, Brother Maynard), Gilliam (Patsy, Green Knight, The Old Man from Scene 24, The Animator), Jones (Sir Bedevere, Old Woman), Palin (Sir Galahad, Dennis, Sir Robin, Father, Monk), Carol Cleveland (Zoot, Dingo)

Cameos: Connie Booth (The Witch, Mrs Cleese), Neil Innes (Minstrel), Maggie Weston (Hand Turning Page, Mrs Gilliam)

Crew: Directors: Gilliam & Jones, Writers: Chapman & Cleese & Gilliam & Idle & Jones & Palin, Producers: Mark Forstater & John Goldstone, Cinematographer: Terry Bedford, Editing: John Hackney, Music: De Wolfe, Songs: Neil Innes, Production Manager: Julian Doyle

The Plot: King Arthur wanders aimlessly around his kingdom, accompanied only by his trusty steed Patsy (who is really a rather shabby retainer with a pair of coconuts). Then God decides to instruct Arthur to search for The Holy Grail. Suitably inspired, Arthur wanders aimlessly around his kingdom, accompanied by an ever-growing cadre of the kingdom's bravest and finest knights (who are really a rather shabby bunch of blowhards and misfits who also have coconuts).

Eventually, after several adventures which seemed no more feasible when John Boorman tried to retell them without the gags in *Excalibur*, Arthur learns the location of The Grail and sets off to claim it, only to learn that the French have got there first. Understandably incensed, Arthur spontaneously assembles a massive army and is about to declare war on France when the police arrive in their squad cars and start arresting people for wandering around the Scottish countryside in silly costumes.

The Thickening: Because Gilliam only directed half of this film, based on the script of his colleagues, *Holy Grail* is only a Gilliam film in the loosest sense. Nevertheless, I am including it because it does carry themes and ideas which will surface repeatedly throughout the rest of his work.

Describing how they divided up the workload, Jones admits: "It's very odd, I think we sort of did it on alternate days, is what I remember, but Terry and I very much agree that we knew what we wanted, and I couldn't tell you who was responsible for what in terms of the look of the thing." [1]

The general consensus among the Pythons seems to have been that allowing them both to direct was a good idea because a) Jones would concentrate on the performances, whilst Gilliam would make it look good, and b) no one else wanted the job. The problems began because of the different working practices which arose from these two demands. Ultimately, the difference between their directing styles came down to one thing – Jones had always been down on the floor with the lads during the rehearsals and shooting, whilst Gilliam had only been an occasional visitor, spending the majority of his time alone in his animation studio. Jones was used to working with people, Gilliam was used to moving bits of paper around.

Cleese was never a fan of hanging around waiting for the technicians: "I remember that Terry G. was lighting a shot with *infinite* care, which meant that we were kneeling there [in full armour] for ages, and he was moving the camera a couple of inches this way, then he'd move it *back* again. I remember complaining after a time, saying, 'Do you realise this is really uncomfortable?' And I certainly realised that he'd been doing all this kind of thing for years in the animation, without the bits of paper complaining to him, and I think it was hard on him at that stage to think of the actors as *people*." [2]

It seems that Gilliam, in hindsight, would concur with that appraisal, since his recollection of the incident is somewhat more straightforward: "[I said] 'Shut up! This is your fucking sketch, you wrote this fucking thing, I don't need this!' And I walked off; the dam finally cracked and I went off in a huff and lay there in the grass: 'I'm not going to do this shit.' It was appalling behaviour! I left Terry to take them on." [3]

From then onwards, Jones worked at directing the cast, whilst Gilliam concentrated on working with the crew. This worked reasonably well...then came the editing. Jones and Gilliam would tussle all day long over which shots should be in and which not, and how the scenes should be paced, and so on, with Jones generally winning. However, the wily American had a cunning plan: "I'd go back late at night and recut what had been done during the day, and he wouldn't notice what I'd done. It was very silly at times..." [4]

Grotesquerie: There are many elements to *Holy Grail* which correspond to the requirements of The Grotesque, and also foreshadow the concerns that Gilliam would go on to explore in greater depth and at more leisure in his own films.

The opening shot is clearly Gilliam. As smoke billows enigmatically across the screen, Arthur and Patsy ride out of the haze. Behind them, we can make out the only other detail, a torture wheel with a skeleton on it. This is lifted from Pieter Bruegel's 1562 vision of Hell *The Triumph Of Death* where a row of such torture wheels line the horizon. This will most definitely not be the last time Gilliam will draw on the macabre works of Bruegel, or his near-contemporary Hieronymus Bosch.

Much later, the Tim the Enchanter scene has a visual splendour which could only come from Gilliam, but the dead give-away is the shot he later adapted for *Time Bandits*, which uses extreme perspective to give the impression that Arthur and his knights are walking out of the nose socket of a human skull. This image perfectly emphasises the feeling of growing dread as the knights approach the certain death which awaits them "with nasty big teeth."

Gilliam's visual flair also survives in the "Bring out your dead" sketch, employing the chilly winter sun to enrich the scene with a colour palette which would not be out of place in a Tarkovsky movie. A considerable contribution to this is the care the Pythons took in making the film feel genuinely medieval. Even if they differed in their approach to filming it, both directors were determined to make their depiction of 932 AD as seriously believable as possible: "We were doing comedy, but we didn't want it to look like light entertainment. I'm not sure how many film-makers before us had taken the sense of place so seriously in comedy..." [5]

The bloodletting of *Jabberwocky*'s tournament is pre-empted in the Black Knight sequence, where Cleese has several limbs unceremoniously cut off to the accompaniment of much spilled blood. Slightly subtler continuations of this brutality appear throughout the film – such as in the fleeting background appearance of three knights skewered on one lance.

There is more bloodletting when the concept of heroism is put under the microscope (much as it is in Gilliam's solo films) through the character of Launcelot who, so fired up by his chance to rescue a 'damsel' in distress, successfully butchers several dozen innocent people.

Later, another favourite Gilliam motif, the decapitation, raises its ugly head during the Cave of Caerbannog scene, where several knights are brutally beheaded by a vicious man-eating fluffy bunny.

The less blood-soaked, but no-less transgressive aspects of grotesquerie are represented here. Take, for example, the point where, whilst continuing on their quest, the knights nobly indulge in a spot of cannibalism, as they are "...forced to eat Robin's minstrels. And there was much rejoicing."

Quotes:
1: Jones quoted in David Morgan, *Monty Python Speaks!*, p117
2: Cleese quoted in ibid p126
3: Gilliam quoted in ibid p127
4: Gilliam quoted in Ian Christie, *Gilliam On Gilliam*, p58
5: ibid

Jabberwocky (1976)

"Why don't you sit back and let something nice happen to you for a change?"

Cast: Michael Palin (Dennis Cooper), John Le Mesurier (Passelewe), Max Wall (King Bruno the Questionable), Deborah Fallender (Princess Rita), Warren Mitchell (Mr Fishfinger), Annette Badland (Griselda Fishfinger), Harry H Corbett (Jules the Squire), Bernard Bresslaw (Fergus the Landlord), John Bird (First Herald), David Prowse (Red Herring Knight and Black Knight)

Cameos: Jones (Poacher), Gilliam (Man With Rock), Brian Glover (Armourer), Rodney Bewes (Other Squire), Neil Innes (Second Herald)

Crew: Director: Gilliam, Writers: Charles Alverson & Gilliam, Producers: Julian Doyle & John Goldstone & Sandy Lieberson, Music: De Wolfe, Cinematographer: Terry Bedford, Make-up: Maggie Weston, Focus Puller: Roger Pratt

The Plot: Dennis Cooper is happy to spend his days ruining his father's Coopery with modernising notions - such as disposable barrels. On his deathbed, his father disowns him so Dennis must head off to The Great Walled City to make his fortune. Pausing only to pledge his troth to the monstrous Griselda (known to her dad as 'Greasy') he sets off.

The world of Flagelot City is very different to that which he knows. The merchants and Guilds have the town sewn up. Because some terrible monster is abroad, all the peasants from the surrounding villages want protection within the city's walls. Therefore, market forces have driven prices so high, the local businessmen have grown fat on the proceeds whilst peasants starve in the streets. Despite the protestations of the merchants, the King decides to offer his daughter's hand as reward to the knight who slays the monster. Dennis is conned into being the squire for the chosen knight.

Of course, Dennis accidentally kills the beastie himself, is swiftly married to the Princess and is dragged off to rule over half the kingdom, all the while begging to be allowed to live unhappily ever after with his beloved Griselda.

The Thickening: Gilliam's decision to begin his solo post-Python career with *Jabberwocky* was, at least in part, motivated by his dissatisfaction with *Holy Grail*: "The approach of Python was slightly different from the way I would approach it, so I wanted to get into those untouched areas." [1]

As with *Holy Grail*, this film evokes a filthy, convincing Dark Ages: "...darker than anyone had thought possible." Yet, where the Python film was just a series of bizarre episodes tenuously hung on the bones of the Arthurian myth, *Jabberwocky* makes some attempt to reflect medieval society as it actually was, a complex social order based around the class system, trade, conquest, poverty, fear and silly hats.

Gilliam didn't want his first solo project to be perceived as just another Python comedy, so he made a concerted efforts to avoid that...by casting Michael Palin. *Jabberwocky* is certainly not an uncomplicated comedy, since it employs infantile scatological farce as readily and unrepentantly as skillful social satire. Of course, Gilliam always had aspirations to do more than just make people laugh, even his earliest animations make you think as often as they make you feel.

Gilliam has stated that he admired the gritty, realistic look of Richard Lester's *Musketeer* films (1973 & 1974), and wished to achieve something like it in *Jabberwocky*. He was never more successful than in the introduction to the royal palace. Passelewe, the King's Chamberlain, prowls through the darkness of an irregular corridor, accompanied by dramatic, suspenseful music. He steps over a Gilliam standby: the cleaning lady on hands and knees, sweeping up the masonry which will continue to fall from the ceiling throughout the film.

Since much of the castle-based footage was shot in the real, unreconstructed interiors of Chepstow and Pembroke castles, Gilliam simply allows the dilapidation to make his point that the English nobility has always been in ruins!

As will become a constant in Gilliam films, the mass media is represented early on, given that the opening narration is actually delivered by The City's resident Punch and Judy Man, who re-enacts the events of the outside world in a heightened and stylised manner. Later, when Dennis is out facing The Jabberwock, the Punch and Judy Man portrays this in a fantasy form, intercut with images of the reality. Gilliam has always been aware of the incongruity between the fantasy stories he wants to tell, and the realities associated with getting them told.

The film also borrows the motifs of other genres, such as the subjective camera shots from the Jabberwock's perspective, which evoke the horror film genre (as well as saving on expensive special effects!) However, the most delicious (ab)use of generic motif, is of the fairy tale, which he mixes with pantomime. The King's daughter is determined to live a fairy-tale fantasy to the hilt, holed up in her tower, surrounded by the Blessed Sisters of Misery: "I'm supposed to marry a Prince. That's why I wait in this tower, just like all the books say to do." Unfortunately for Dennis and his beloved Greasy, heroes in fairy tales must have preordained happy endings. He is forcibly married and sent off to claim half of the Princess...sorry, half of the kingdom. Again and again, throughout this book, we will see Gilliam return to this theme of the misapprehension and inappropriateness of 'heroism.'

Celebrating the grand tradition of British farce, Dennis must dress as a nun to escape the castle. But it is typical of Gilliam's view of the world, that Sister Jessica, from whom Dennis gets the habit, is also actually a man in drag. This skewed view of bedroom farce, also informs the death of Jules The Squire, an inveterate hedonist who meets his end (so to speak) crushed beneath the marital bed of the landlord he had been busily cuckolding. Both Harry H Corbett and, more frequently, Bernard Bresslaw, had served their time in the *Carry On* films, to which such scenes were meat and veg.

You can't deny that Gilliam has a dynamic range of influences - it spans the paintings of Pieter Bruegel *and* the films of Gerald Thomas!

Grotesquerie: Jabberwocky was an antidote to the romanticised depictions of the Dark Ages as seen in movies from *The Adventures Of Robin Hood* (1938) to *Camelot* (1967). Partly because, unlike most movies set in that period, it was actually shot in miserable old England not on the sun-kissed hills of Southern California.

Hobbes memorably described the Dark Ages as being a time of "...continual fear and danger of violent death; and the life of man, solitary, poor, nasty, brutish, and short." [2] If there was one vision of the period Gilliam wanted to represent, this would be it! Never one to hide his influences, he opens the movie with a montage of apocalyptic details from Pieter Bruegel the Elder's *The Triumph Of Death (1562)* and *Tower Of Babel* (1563). "[*Jabberwocky* is] probably as close to their paintings as any film I've ever seen, actually...We set the scene quite seriously [as we did in *Holy Grail*]...I think the best comedy comes out of a sense of reality. It's a combination of reality and either surrealism or absurdity mixing." [3]

Indeed, one commentator was moved to note: "...it can be no accident that *Jabberwocky* bears almost no relation to Lewis Carroll, but turns out to be instead an uncannily persuasive Bruegelesque portrait of the Middle Ages with many slyly snide side glances at the modern day." [4]

The illustrations are numerous. Gilliam dwells constantly on the squalor of the environment, and that, combined with the undisguised frailties of his characters, offers him the most opportunities for grotesquerie and lavatorial humour. How does Dennis make it into the impenetrable Walled City? One of the sentries is caught short and nips into the bushes, so Dennis just wanders past. How very human.

Inside, we are introduced to city life without the oft-ignored miracle of plumbing. Mud and excrement cohabit at an intimate level with the milling crowds. The laughter these scenes elicit is of relief, of simple gratitude that we now live in a PC world (that's Post Crapper).

Other examples of grotesquerie are so numerous, a simple list will suffice. Mr Fishfinger opens the film, proudly sporting a fine set of greenish-brown teeth. Surely the next great fashion accessory! His delightful daughter, Griselda has all the grace and charm of your average hippopotamus, whilst her little brother, Roger, pisses all over Dennis as soon as he sees him. This is not the last time Dennis will be so blessed. Says it all, really. 'The' Wat Dabney becomes the precursor for *Life Of Brian*'s ex-leper, by sawing off a foot so he can beg and make some kind of living. Cannibalism and auto-cannibalism are two areas grotesquerie delights in. One beggar, in appealing to the King, proudly announces that he was so hungry he "...ate three toes off my...ehm...right foot!" Later, when Dennis escapes the King's clutches, Bruno decides that the Landlord must have eaten him, and slams him up for the night. Out in the sticks, skeletons are becoming ever-more prevalent. One of the brigands Dennis and the Knight come across wears a cow skull for a hat. Next, they pass through a burned-out village, piled with charred body parts. The jarring, suspenseful music makes this sequence genuinely disturbing, and therefore distracts your attention away from what comes next - the ultimate juvenile shit joke – as later borrowed by Ringo Starr's *Caveman* (1981) and Spielberg's *Jurassic Park* (1993).

The Jabberwock itself is the most grotesque of all creatures - a Chimera. It is an unholy mixture of ragged exo-skeleton, bristling with horns and a beak with punctured leathery wings and a tail, all built around the frame of a five-ton turkey.

Inversions And Transformations: When his beloved Greasy tosses a rotten potato out of the window, Dennis catches it, considering it a love token. It is really just her garbage. Later, when Dennis arrives at the gate of the starving Great Walled City, this rotten potato actually becomes a valuable object. Later still, it starts to germinate in Dennis' pocket. So, thinking about it, a potato isn't really that bad a symbol of growing love.

The ancient King is depicted as a shrivelled-up baby, wearing his nappy and bonnet, and carrying his mitre like a rattle. He is endlessly indulged by his nanny, Passelewe.

When they take Dennis prisoner, we see that The Flagellants view the world in a substantially different way from even their medieval counterparts. They don't think it fair that Dennis should get all the 'bone-crushing horror' their catapult has to offer. So one of the Flagellants determinedly goes first - setting himself alight and hurling himself over the castle walls, for pure personal satisfaction. Takes all sorts.

Fantasies: Dennis Cooper is that rarest of creatures in a Gilliam film, a protagonist with no imagination. His dreams are small and delusional. He wants to modernise his father's business, but doesn't know why. He wants to marry the monstrous Griselda, presumably because he believes he *must* marry, and she is the only woman available. One wonders why. His dearest wish is to make a modest living (as a stocktaker of some sort) so he can support Griselda in the deplorable manner to which she is accustomed. Instead he has a fantasy of grandiose proportions thrust upon him, involving the slaying of a beast, the winning of a princess and riches beyond the wildest dreams he never actually had.

Princess Rita is the most traditionally Gilliamesque character, determined to pursue a vision in the face of convention, good sense, all available evidence and the laws of physics: "Deborah Fallender...gives the character such conviction as a girl stoned out of her mind on fairy tale legend, that one is terrified that someone will try to disillusion her." [5] When Dennis stumbles into her room, she is so enraptured by him, convinced he is her Prince that she doesn't notice the untimely arrival of her *real* prince.

King Bruno has dreams. He imagines the great, noble, Arthurian traditions might one day be applied to his grotty little kingdom. He envisions a great, spectacular tournament. What he gets instead, involves a lot of mud and blood and very little dignity. He imagines his castle as the location for valiant deeds. What he gets is plaster in his soup and a tower that demonstrates comedic timing by collapsing on cue.

Otherwise, there is a lot of dreamlike falling imagery in this film, all seemingly inspired by The Bridge of Death scene from *Holy Grail*: a tournament knight rebounds off a wall and falls on his head; a flagellant fires himself over the battlements; and the Black Knight falls to his death, hurled by The Jabberwock.

Bureaucracies: Bureaucracies exist to suppress the lowly man by organising his life for him. As such, the British class system and the politics those at the top of it espouse, form the ultimate bureaucracy.

The fledgling policies of monetarism which would go on to lay waste to the 80s (and inspire *The Crimson Permanent Assurance*) are reflected here: The only way through the gate into The Great Walled City, is to bring some money for them to take off you. Capitalism cannot survive without financially well-endowed victims on which to prey.

The merchant uses accountants' logic to emphasise the positive aspects of any atrocity: "In the long term, it will be shown that we owe to the monster a period of prosperity unprecedented in this kingdom!" This deliberate maintenance of a politically-expedient siege is similar, in motive, to *Brazil*'s phantom terrorist bombings and *Baron Munchausen*'s Turkish siege.

When out on the road, Dennis single-handedly saves his beloved Griselda and her family from brigands, but all they can see is the impotent, prone figure of the knight. Because heroism is not the province of his class, Dennis is completely ignored.

Be Headings: Throughout Gilliam's work, there is a disturbing trend towards images of decapitation, of separating the head from the body, and tearing back the flesh to reveal the skull beneath. The film begins with Gilliam getting his own back on Terry Jones for their experiences co-directing *Holy Grail* – he has him killed in a most messy and protracted manner by the unseen Jabberwock. The beast leaves behind a steaming skeleton, dripping with blood and slivers of undigested meat, with a completely intact head.

King Bruno has the first herald swiftly and ignominiously decapitated. After this, the severed head is kicked about by the King and half-nelsoned by a guard.

Finally, as proof of his glorious victory, Dennis brings home the head – just like Agamemnon will in *Time Bandits*.

Quotes:
1: Gilliam quoted in Anne Thompson, *Film Comment*, Nov-Dec 1981, p51
2: Thomas Hobbes. *Leviathan*, i, xiii
3: Gilliam quoted in Anne Thompson, *Film Comment*, p51
4: Alan Brien quoted in John O Thompson, *Monty Python's Complete And Utter Theory Of The Grotesque*, p6
5: Alexander Stuart, *Films and Filming*, June 1977, p39

Part Two: The Three Ages Of Man

Time Bandits (1981)

"I think it's something to do with free will!"

Cast: Craig Warnock (Kevin Lotterby), David Rappaport (Randall), Jack Purvis (Wally), Kenny Baker (Fidgit), Mike Edmonds (Og), Malcolm Dixon (Strutter), Tiny Ross (Vermin), Ian Holm (Napoleon), Sean Connery (Agamemnon), David Warner (Evil), Peter Vaughan (Winston the Ogre), Katherine Helmond (Mrs Ogre), Sir Ralph Richardson (The Supreme Being)

Cameos: Charles McKeown (Theatre Manager), Shelley Duvall (Pansy), Palin (Vincent), Cleese (Robin Hood), Winston Dennis (Minotaur), Jim Broadbent (Gameshow Host), Myrtle Devenish (Beryl, the Gameshow Contestant)

Crew: Director: Gilliam, Writers: Palin & Gilliam, Producers: Gilliam & George Harrison & Denis O'Brien, Cinematographer: Peter Biziou, Editor: Julian Doyle, Music: Mike Moran, Song: George Harrison

The Plot: Kevin is an imaginative, inquisitive child, crushed by emotionless parents. Then, one evening, a knight in full armour riding a horse bursts out of his wardrobe. Soon after, six rather shabby looking dwarves appear - they are keepers of the map which locates all holes in time, one of which is in Kevin's wardrobe. The six are being pursued through time by The Supreme Being (known as God to his friends) and accidentally take Kevin along with them.

Their first port of call is Castiglione as Napoleon is endeavouring to destroy it. Their intent? Rob him blind of all the cities riches and scarper to the Middle Ages. This they do, but end up in Sherwood Forest where Robin Hood relieves them of their booty and redistributes it among the poor. Undeterred, they make their way to ancient Mycenae to burgle Agamemnon's court.

After a brief stop-off on the Titanic, their greed for The Most Valuable Object In The World leads them to The Time Of Legends and into the clutches of Evil in his mighty Fortress Of Ultimate Darkness.

The Thickening: For Kevin's parents, acquisition is the purpose of life. Father balefully gazes at *Exchange & Mart* whilst mother bleats on about the neighbour's rotisserie. Both spend their evenings sitting catatonic on plastic-wrapped seats in front of a television they don't actually watch. The *Your Money Or Your Life* game show was, at the time, a cutting satire of American-style television. Of course, 20 years on, in a post- *Pets Win Prizes* and *National Lobotomy* Britain, drowning members of your family in custard in return for your 15 minutes of fame, seems positively tame. Media, Gilliam believes, dulls the senses and robs us of our dreams: "I find that a lot of kids don't read; so I don't know where they're getting their myths or their ideas from. Unless it's from television and movies, which are very limited compared with what books have to offer." [1]

Kevin is overloaded with myths and ideas. To counteract his mundane real life, his mind flies to worlds of wars and knights. It is not insignificant that, whilst his parents vegetate in front of the glass teat he sits with his back to it, his head buried in a book. Up in his room his imagination has full sway. When the dwarves arrive they comment that this room is "Not on the map." But it has a map of its own, played out across its carpet and walls - the adventures he is about to embark on, and most particularly, the architecture of The Fortress, are all foreshadowed in the cowboys and tanks, the chessboard and Lego bricks.

Gilliam felt like making a film children could particularly enjoy, something which was entirely impossible within the confines of Python, and settled upon the same motif which Steven Spielberg was about to employ on the other side of the Atlantic for his film *ET* (1982) – the idea of keeping the camera down at a child's eye level throughout. However, Gilliam was concerned that one short person would find it difficult to carry such a film, so Gilliam opted to make the bandits short as well. From that, everything else flowed.

Following on from *Jabberwocky*'s fairy-tale roots, Gilliam has very definite views on fiction aimed at children: "I think the purpose of the fairy tale is to give a rather frightening experience...it says there are less than wonderful things in the world, that there's evil out there, there's dangerous things, and I think it builds the kid's strength up in an interesting way, rather than *Sesame Street*, which says that everybody's lovely and the world's a wonderful place. I don't believe that." [2]

One of the tasks Gilliam and Palin set themselves here, again following on from their work in *Jabberwocky*, was the exploding of images of heroes. Firstly, of course, there are the bandits. Exemplifying the free spirit of the oppressed peoples of the world, they are real working-class heroes, yet they are quite astonishingly awful, both to each other and to anyone else who happens to cross their path.

Kevin clearly admires and is intimidated by the legend which precedes Napoleon and yet, in person, the great man is insecure, petty and height-obsessed. Robin Hood, far from being the dashing hero of myth and legend is, in reality, a condescending upper-class twit. We are not intended to take these figures literally - after all, they speak modern English just as they would in a child's dream. They exist purely for their iconic significance, and so we can see them being eroded by their simple human frailties.

It is not accidental that the dwarves arrive in Castiglione through the backstage area of a theatre. As we will see again in *Munchausen*, the theatre is a microcosm of life, all flats and cables and sandbags, hidden away in order to make magic out front. By debunking heroes and myths, Gilliam is showing the ropes and weights behind the flat lies we tell kids.

Indeed, all the authority figures here, from Kevin's parents upwards, are dealt with mercilessly. The only partial exception are the two roles played by Sean Connery: Agamemnon and the fireman. Connery was mentioned by name in the script: "Agamemnon removes his helmet to reveal...Sean Connery (or an actor of equal but cheaper stature)!" He was the most iconically heroic actor Gilliam and Palin could think of.

By lampooning icons such as these, Gilliam is saying that you should never trust the outward appearance of things. Even the sainted Agamemnon, the wise and noble leader, the 'good father' Kevin so desperately craves, is not immune to the rigours of a dysfunctional family. There is clearly no direct communication between him and his understandably disgruntled wife.

Once in The Time Of Legends (the source of all the myths that have been handed down to children like Kevin for centuries) he finds that disappointment will pursue him still. Just as the heroes don't live up to expectation, neither do the monsters. They meet a middle-aged, rheumatic Ogre who looks upon scaring people as more of a job than a vocation.

Increasingly, those simple human frailties to which even dwarf gardeners are prone, begin to tell and the bandits' greed becomes ambitious. They decide to go after The Most Fabulous Object In The World, not realising that they already have the most fabulous object: the map! And so the dwarves are caged by their own greed. In exactly the kind of cage we will see in *Brazil*'s dreams and on *Munchausen*'s Moon. Indeed, escaping the metaphorical cage of conformity will be a constant theme throughout Gilliam's subsequent films, if not of his whole life!

It is at this point when the flip side of the appearances-can-be-deceiving argument comes in to play. Og is allegedly the dumbest of the dwarves, yet it was he who unleashed his imagination to devise the entirely unprecedented tree, The Pink Bungadoo: "Six hundred feet high, bright red, and smelled terrible..." It is he who picks the lock of their prison. This, then, permits the hitherto self-obsessed gang to begin

31

to operate like a team, saving themselves in the most spectacularly show-offish fashion. These short, snotty, rude vagabonds are the real heroes, not the figures of myth and legend. They then underscore this new-found if ill-fitting status by returning with reinforcements when Kevin and Og take on Evil.

And so The Supreme Being (whom we shall henceforth refer to as TSB) finally consents to take a hand. He and Evil never get to cross verbal wits because TSB simply destroys Evil before manifesting. Indeed, the TSB scene is pretty much a one-hander, with the dwarves automatically resuming their subservient position and Kevin being sidelined.

The scene we see is not as it was written, but was heavily reworked by Richardson. The idea of posting the fragments of Evil into a post box was Richardson's, and he also had final say over his own dialogue with the emphatic and dead-pan insistence: "God wouldn't say that!" Since Sir Ralph was about as close to God as most of the assembly had ever come, they couldn't really argue.

However, even with the arrival of the one with whom the buck absolutely stops – the film's message that heroes will always let you down, is not forgotten. TSB is a woolly thinker, but he isn't the binary opposite of Evil, he isn't simple undisputed Good. He is officious and distant and seemingly has no interest in the minutiae of running a universe.

Kevin, disappointed, decides to chide TSB: "You mean you let all those people die, just to test your creation?"

"Yes."

Kevin then follows this with the kind of question that children excel at asking, and which Philosophy has spent several thousand years failing to answer: "Why do we have to have Evil?"

"I think it's something to do with free will!" Even TSB isn't entirely sure.

And so Kevin has come to the end of this stage in his journey. But, is the journey over? TSB's "He must stay and continue the fight" and the chip off the old Evil block which escapes detection, suggest not. TSB made Evil, and therefore he must be in the position of making Good. Kevin, it seems, has inadvertently been auditioning for the role. So, if this is all a dream, then this is his path to becoming the kind of hero he admires – the universal torch-bearer of Good.

Kevin's days of needing guidance and heroes are over. As he awakes back into the blazing inferno his parents' gadgets have made of their house, he is rescued by a far more tangible manifestation of Sean Connery the hero, this time as the fireman. This implies that real heroes, and real good fathers, are out there somewhere.

And so the films ends jarringly, with Kevin left alone, standing on his lawn, homeless, gazing in shock at the smouldering ashes of his parents. But he no longer needs them. He has crossed his personal rubicon, he has a photograph of the map, several centuries of experience behind him, and a chunk of Evil to battle against. Everything, in other words, a growing boy needs. This was Gilliam's intention: "I felt he was now capable of looking after himself in life - not only because he had been through this adventure, but also because he had discovered that heroes are not usually what they're cracked up to be." [3]

Grotesquerie: Given that this film was for children, Gilliam is remarkably restrained for the first half hour or so, only giving vent to his naturally scatological sense of humour with the bandits' arrival in The Middle Ages. This sequence follows on directly from *Jabberwocky* in its gruesome, muddy visualisation (much as the Mycenae sequence seems initially like an out-take from *Life Of Brian*) even to the extent of beginning as *Jabberwocky* finished, with Michael Palin and his lady in a coach.

The Fortress of Ultimate Darkness, seems to have been inspired in equal measure by Bruegel's chaotic paintings *Tower Of Babel* and *Little Tower Of Babel* (both 1563) as well as HR Giger's bio-mechanical paintings of *New York* (1980). Evil himself wears a headdress clearly influenced by the cables and bones which went into Giger's designs for Ridley Scott's *Alien* (1979).

The deserts of The Time Of Legends which they wander across, are introduced by a close-up of an animal skull. As Randall walks blithely through a giant ribcage, we are reminded of Dennis picking his way through the skeleton-strewn quarry of the Jabberwock, but also of the two androids shuffling across the Tattooine wastes in *Star Wars* (1977), one of whom, of course, was portrayed by Kenny Baker. This sequence comes to a climax when Randall picks up a human skull and hurls it at Wally, missing him completely and shattering Evil's Invisible Barrier. That's using your head!

Inversions And Transformations: The stop-off points in the bandits' journey were chosen by Gilliam and Palin because of their starkly contrasting nature: the open fields and ruins of Castiglione; the claustrophobic wilds of rain-soaked Sherwood Forest; the sun-parched expanses of the Mycenae deserts; the subarctic wastes of the North Atlantic; and finally The Time of Legends where almost everything that preceded it is represented in one form or another.

The vehicle of being spirited away on a travelling adventure by a crowd of dwarves is a direct inversion of one of the films which most inspired Gilliam: Alexander Korda's *Thief Of Bagdad* (1940), where a vastly proportioned giant takes a young boy on magical adventures.

There is much contrasting short with tall here, using such elaborate and expensive techniques as getting the tall actors to stand on boxes or the small actors to sit down. Yet, whilst this visual anachronism is never off-screen no one, barring the height-obsessed Napoleon, ever seems to notice how short they are. It is simply taken as read.

Evil is capable of grotesque transformation, as he first inflates into a giant pincushion, then leaves his biological state behind altogether as he turns into a giant mechanical roundabout. Ultimately, Evil's megalomania amounts to nothing more than a simple, mundane desire to reverse the order of things: "We will turn mountains into seas, turn skies into rivers, and the fjords into deserts, and the deserts into quagmire!"

Of course, in The Time Of Legends where Evil has reign, inverted is exactly how everything is. To get there, the dwarves fall upwards out of the ocean, before rising back down into it, whilst the image turns briefly into a negative and their suits switch from black to white. Once there, the first locals they encounter are Mr and Mrs Ogre, for whom the grotesque is considered desirable. He complains bitterly about anti-pollution campaigners who have ensured that he can now only catch fish in his nets, not the old boots he prefers. Finally, the film ends with the reverse of its beginning: a pull back out to the extremes of the map (not unlike that which opens Robert Zemeckis' *Contact* or closes Barry Sonnenfeld's *Men In Black* [both 1997]). The map is then rolled up and taken away, framing the film with the traditional fairy-tale-style convention, as demonstrated with the hand turning the pages in *Holy Grail* and, for that matter, with *Star Wars*' celebrated 'A long time ago in a galaxy far, far away.'[TM]

Fantasies: As Kevin lies on his bed awaiting what new delights his wardrobe has to offer him, he slips off to sleep. This, then sets up the traditional children's fiction finale: 'And then I woke up!' As the satchel full of photos indicate, it is too simplistic to put his adventures down as simply a dream, yet they are redolent with dream logic and dream imagery. This will very definitely not be the last time a Gilliam protagonist is confused about the reality of what he has seen.

When he is first pulled out of his own reality, the dwarves open up a corridor into the fourth dimension and then promptly fall off the end. This will be the first of many plummets they make. As with the dreams of the anxious mind, there is a lot of falling and fear of falling, here. This concern will be shared by Sam Lowry in *Brazil*.

Bureaucracies: Like the rigid class structure of *Jabberwocky*, Gilliam can't resist the temptation to comment on the British obsession with hierarchy. Consequently, the root cause of everything which happens in *Time Bandits* is the fact that Heaven is organised along bureaucratic lines, much like The Civil Service, with TSB as the notional minister: "He made all the big stuff like good and evil, men and women, night and day..." The dwarves had the dirty jobs: "We did trees and shrubs." Then they found themselves demoted to Maintenance, a necessary task because, as with anything designed by committee, the universe is full of holes: "To be quite frank, Kevin, the fabric of the universe is far from perfect. It was a bit of a botch job, y'see; we only had seven days to make it."

It is probably wise, at this point, to mention that the first draft of *Brazil* (which was, at one point, going to be called *The Ministry*) was already written, before Gilliam began work on *Time Bandits*. Therefore, the evils of a civil-service-style bureaucratic structure was already at the forefront of Gilliam's mind. Consequently, his sympathy lies entirely with the bandits, warts and all, and TSB comes across as a distant, somewhat callous demagogue, who has created Evil purely...because he can. TSB's entire rationale is purely to put Evil through a feasibility study: "I had to have some way of testing my handiwork. I think it turned out rather well, don't you!?" And there, in his absence of motive, lies the similarity between TSB and his creation, Evil, they both expend their power arbitrarily because there is no one to tell them otherwise.

Be Headings: The Supreme Being pursues the bandits through time in the form of a giant disembodied head, shrouded in cloud and bellowing at them. Not unlike, it must be noted, The Great and Powerful Oz from *The Wizard Of Oz* (1939). In keeping with this, when TSB emerges from all his smoke and thunder, he is really just an ordinary little grey-haired man.

The Minotaur is clearly a man wearing a mouldy, moth-eaten bull's head, held on with straps and buckles – implying that the monster of myth and legend, was no more than a convincing trick. Agamemnon has a fearsome full-head helmet, which he removes to reveal the man inside.

Quotes:

1: Gilliam quoted in the audio commentary to the *Criterion Collection* DVD of *Time Bandits*
2: Gilliam quoted in Anne Thompson, *Film Comment*, p50
3: Gilliam quoted in the *Time Bandits FAQ* of the *Dreams* website

The Crimson Permanent Assurance (1983)

"It's fun to charter an accountant, and sail the wide accountant sea."

Cast: Sydney Arnold, Eric Francis, Billy John, Russell Kilmister, Len Marten, John Scott Martin, Larry Noble, Paddy Ryan, Leslie Sarony, Ronald Shilling, Wally Thomas, Albert Welch, (The Brits) Guy Bertrand, Andrew Bicknell, Ross Davidson, Tim Douglas, Peter Mantle, Peter Merrill, Cameron Miller, Eric Stovell, Jack Armstrong, Robert Carrick, (The Americans) Myrtle Devenish (Tea Lady), Matt Frewer (Sword-Wielding American), Gareth Milne (Out Of Window American)
Cameos: Gilliam & Palin (Window Cleaners), Chapman & Jones (The Americans)
Crew: Director: Gilliam, Writer: Gilliam, Producer: John Goldstone, Cinematographer: Roger Pratt, Editor: Julian Doyle, Music: John DuPrez, Shanty: Idle

The Plot: The put-upon old men of the Permanent Assurance Company finally snap and rebel against their American corporate oppressors. They change from gentle old accountants to murderous pirates. Slipping its high street anchor, their stately old Edwardian building sets sail and attacks the mighty corporations of Wall Street. They lay waste to the bastions of Monetarism then sail off into the horizon, the edge of which they promptly drop off.

The Thickening: This 16 minute short feature was initially intended to be an animated sequence in the body of *Monty Python's Meaning Of Life*, which Gilliam would go off and do by himself, as usual. However, wishing to put his animating days behind him (apart from the ubiquitous *Python* title sequence), Gilliam decided that he would rather repeat his working practice for the spaceship sequence in *Monty Python's Life Of Brian*, by going off into his own little studio, with his own little crew, and making *The Crimson Permanent Assurance* as a live-action segment.

Pirates were obviously at the forefront of people's minds in those early years of Thatcherism, as Chapman, Idle and Cleese were also preparing to appear in *Yellowbeard* (1983). Consequently, no one foresaw a problem with Gilliam's request because it would get him out from under their feet. Gilliam made occasional visits to the set of *Monty Python's Meaning Of Life*, to dress up as Marie-Antoinette or have his liver removed, but mostly he worked away, in secret, on his own little segment.

Then he started asking for more money.

Jones, busily directing the main feature, demonstrates a trace of envy when recollecting the process: "...it was only when we heard that Terry wanted *another* million dollars, or whatever it was, we suddenly realised it was a whole different feature going on! We kept going to his studio next door, and he had these *huge* sets compared to what we had." [1]

Gilliam freely admits that things were getting out of hand: "When I approached it, I thought it would be a piece of cake...nobody took it seriously until it was too late. Then they realised they had something as complicated as the entire rest of the film." [2]

However, the real problems became apparent during the editing, when they realised that, no matter how much Gilliam cut it back, the sequence wouldn't fit into the main body of the film. The differences in lighting and set design stopped it blending in, and the pacing was all wrong. So the decision was made to run *The Crimson Permanent Assurance* as a short before the main film. Looking at it now, it is difficult to imagine how it could ever have been thought of otherwise.

Of course, this wasn't in any way Gilliam's devious little plan all along. No. "...The great thing with *Python* was that we were able to do this, to have that kind of freedom to just pull things apart completely, change the shape..." [3]

Like he gave them a choice.

Gilliam was fulfilling his unrealised desire from *Time Bandits*, to do a pirate movie except, being Gilliam, he turned the idea on its head and made them corporate pirates. Because he insisted on giving the film a political as well as satirical edge, it shares many themes with *Brazil*, which was already well into preparation by this point.

With equal parts of Python's *Hell's Grannies* and the notions of old age which would later be expressed in *Munchausen*, the little old men of The Permanent Assurance stage a very un-English uprising. Time to take on the multinationals.

The pirates swing in through the windows, in a manner made popular by the SAS, and not dissimilar to that employed by *Brazil*'s Ministry of Information storm troopers. In doing so, they completely ignore the workmen outside, beavering away cleaning that mountain of windows. One is put in mind of the cleaning lady who becomes inadvertently embroiled in the showdown between Tuttle's forces and the soldiers of the MOI, during one of *Brazil*'s climaxes.

And so, the element of surprise, combined with good old-fashioned brute force, wins the day and the Crimson Permanent Assurance sails off into the sunset, leaving the multinationals in ruins in its wake "...their assets stripped, their policies in tatters."

Inversions And Transformations: Since they worked together on *Jabberwocky*, Gilliam had persistently encouraged his friend Roger Pratt, to stop fannying about behind the camera and make the jump to Director of Photography. He finally succeeded with this short, and the first tangible reward for his faith in his friend can be seen when the sweatshop transforms briefly into a literal slave galley: The rich visual texture of this sequence sets the scene for *all* the Gilliam films which followed.

Resurrecting the Dunkirk spirit, this motley crew of octogenarians swiftly assemble makeshift weapons by attaching a date stamp to a letter spike to make a dagger, or by ripping the blades off the overhead fan to use as swords. This is all so wonderfully feasible, then, best of all, they convert filing cabinets into cannons by the simple expedient of lighting their fuses. Bugs Bunny would have been proud of that one!

The greatest single transformation, however, is when the film shifts gear from the inventively slapstick, to the out-and-out surreal. We leave the plausible well and truly behind as the anchor is drawn from the ground and the building actually begins to move.

Fantasies: This is the first trademark Gilliam moment: when someone yells "Weigh anchor," the grand music dips in tempo and an unlikely tale becomes pure fantasy. Being British, the passers-by accept the huge chain sunk into the pavement, and calmly walk around it without comment. Indeed, they hardly seem to even notice it until it starts to tear the pavement up as the anchor is slowly, agonisingly, ripped from its concrete moorings.

As the building slips its foundations and sails off through The City, the narration resumes with triumph: "And so The Crimson Permanent Assurance was launched upon the high seas of international finance."

This wouldn't be a Gilliam film if opinion wasn't divided over its ending. Here the building heads for the horizon and then falls off the edge. "...while the narrator intones that it *would* have destroyed all the corporations, only the pirates hadn't taken into account their wrong theory of the shape of the world. You figure it out; is it pure surreal whimsy, or does it refer to the antiquated theories and means of The [political] Left in the modern era?" [4]

Well, since the exact words of the narration are: "...[they would have taken on more multinationals] if certain *modern* theories concerning the shape of the world had not proved disastrously wrong." (My emphasis.) I believe that this film is simply demonstrating that, all things which are 'modernised,' are not necessarily 'improved.'

Alternatively, in keeping with the message of *Time Bandits* and *Brazil*, a more complex reading would be to acknowledge that, if you embrace the logic of fantasy and regress into nostalgia, you have to accept the repercussions of that decision. Fantasy is no substitute for Reality, just an alternative to it; and when the one infests the other, the end result is not always pleasant.

Bureaucracies: The sharply dressed American slave masters carry clipboards headed 'The Very Big Corporation of America,' which makes clear Gilliam's attitude towards the corporate imperialism of his fellow countrymen. But, for those who need a tad more explanation, the introductory narration, a common device for setting the scene in historical epics, explains: "In the bleak days of 1983, as England languished in the doldrums of a ruinous monetarist policy, the good, loyal men of The Permanent Assurance Company...strained under the yoke of their oppressive new corporate management."

In model shots which serve as a dry run for the tenement dream sequences Gilliam planned for *Brazil*; the Crimson Permanent Assurance sails down the imposing avenues of glass towers which constitute Wall Street. This vision emerged again when Gilliam got the chance to shoot *The Fisher King* in the real New York, and use its actual skyscrapers to create their own sense of foreboding doom.

Quotes:
1: Jones quoted in David Morgan, *Monty Python Speaks*, pp218-19
2: Gilliam quoted in Kim 'Howard' Johnson, *The First 200 Years Of Monty Python*, p216
3: Gilliam quoted in David Morgan, *Monty Python Speaks*, pp218-19
4: Fred Glass, *Laugh At Obstacles*, *Jump Cut 29*, p12

Brazil (1985)

"Tomorrow was another day."

Cast: Jonathan Pryce (Sam Lowry), Kim Greist (Jill Layton), Robert De Niro (Harry Tuttle), Katherine Helmond (Ida Lowry), Palin (Jack Lint), Ian Holm (Kurtzmann), Bob Hoskins (Spoor), Ian Richardson (Warren), Peter Vaughan (Helpmann), Jim Broadbent (Dr Jaffe)

Cameos: Ray Cooper (Fly-Swatting Technician), Gordon Kaye (MOI Lobby Porter), Winston Dennis (Samurai), Gilliam (Lurker on Stairs), Jack Purvis (Dr Chapman), Charles McKeown (Harvey Lime), Myrtle Devenish (Lint's Secretary), Holly Gilliam (Holly Lint)

Crew: Director: Gilliam, Writers: Gilliam & Charles McKeown & Tom Stoppard & Charles Alverson (uncredited), Producers: Arnon Milchan & Patrick Cassavetti, Cinematographer: Roger Pratt, Editor: Julian Doyle, Music: Michael Kamen

The Plot: Sam Lowry is a minor functionary in a very large Ministry, and he's happy to leave it that way. Leading a boring, workaday life, only ever letting loose in his exquisitely realised dreams. Then, one day, the girl of his dreams appears in the real, waking world.

Sam becomes obsessed with meeting her and decides to use his mother's powerful contacts to get him deeper into The Ministry, so he can have access to the girl's private files.

Increasingly, the lines between his heroic fantasies and his cowardly real-life persona begin to blur. Sam finds himself involved with a renegade plumber, Harry Tuttle, and the case of the man who was tortured to death in his stead – Harry Buttle.

Eventually, as Sam works his way into the confidence of Jill, the girl of his dreams, The Ministry bears down on them both...

The Thickening: At one point in *Time Bandits*, Evil waxes lyrical about how he is going to remake the world in his own image. Well, by the time we get to *Brazil*, he'd made a pretty good job of it!

There is no doubting that *Brazil* is Gilliam's densest, most visually and intellectually challenging film. As he, himself, confesses: "It's not an easy film...It's relentless, it never stops. I was really shocked when I saw it again, a few weeks ago...I wouldn't make it that way now. It was clearly another guy who made that, and I'm not sure I like it." [1]

Well, whether he likes it or not, *Brazil* has become the definitive Gilliam film. Everything prior leads to it, everything since follows from it. Fact is, I could fill this entire book, twice over, with just this one film. And is Gilliam sympathetic? Is he buggery: "People have compared it to: *Citizen Kane*, *One Flew Over The Cuckoo's Nest*, *A Clockwork Orange*, *Dr. Strangelove*...It makes it very difficult for people who are writing articles, when they only have so many words to tell the world what it's all about. It's very difficult, and I'm *not* going to make your life any easier." [2]

As with *Time Bandits*, *Brazil* begins with a television attempting to sell you something that you don't really need. Later, Gilliam foreshadows *Munchausen*'s opening, with a blinding array of dishonest posters – which sell you a mindset, if not a product: 'Happiness, we're all in it together,' 'Don't suspect a friend, report him.' Whilst these form the front line in the argument that *Brazil* owes much of its content to *1984*, (where Gilliam would argue they are more to do with the uniformity of the post-war America in which he was raised) they also serve to help create a passive, consenting populous; a hegemony.

"Gilliam is a migrant, 'America bombards you with dreams and deprives you of your own,' he says, and *Brazil* is about that too: the struggle between private, personal dreams (flying, love) and the great mass-produced fantasies (eternal youth, material wealth, power)." [3]

Of course, this was also one of the pilot themes of *Time Bandits*. In looking at the relation the two films bore to each other, Gilliam was portentous whilst making it: "It's a strange thing, but I think the character Jonathan Pryce plays in *Brazil* is like the boy in *Time Bandits* fifteen years later. He has the same problems, he still dreams, but he's a bit older and things have changed. If I were making a trilogy, this would be part of it." [4] This, then, is the thread that unites his 'Three Ages of Man' trilogy.

Sam's tale is set against a background of blinding technological complexity which simply doesn't work. When we are introduced to him, his electrics are "up the spout again," his beautifully designed wake-up device manages to confuse the relatively simple tasks of toasting bread and pouring coffee. Then his thermostat goes. In-between times, a simple typing error has ramifications which spread through The System, throwing up innumerable clerical errors, not to mention an accidental murder.

The real enemy of free thought and expression is not the jobsworth mentality which keeps The System trundling along, but the worn-down, dysfunctional technology itself. Harry Tuttle's form of counter-attack is to repair the machines. His rebellion is the most dangerous of all – he is efficient. He genuinely believes we are "all in it together, kid," and wants to make 'it' work. His punishment of Spoor and Dowser for undoing his good work at Sam's flat, is fun, but fails to regain Sam his property, so it, as with Tuttle's entire raison d'être, is ultimately futile.

Grotesquerie: In Sam's dream, the Forces of Darkness, who symbolise the storm troopers he sees every day, are ragged, skeletal, dead creatures with artificial baby-face masks, pretending they're something they're not. They form the bridge between Evil's skeletal demons in *Time Bandits* and The Grim Reaper from *Munchausen*. They are the only real opportunity Gilliam has, in this movie, to get all medieval. For the rest of the film, given its pseudo-modern, urban setting, he has to employ a little more subtext and symbolism than previously.

As with any of his films, the symbols are open to interpretation, and there are as many interpretations as there are interpreters: "I'm not certain if these images are analysable on a Freudian level or not; because I don't recognise most of these images as meaning something. Now, maybe that means I've repressed these things so much, they're so deep. But, on the other hand, I think a lot of them are just cute ideas that I've had." [5]

Well, let's see, shall we...

In the film's opening seconds, we have the breakdown of conventional temporal unity: '8.49 PM. Somewhere in the 20th century.' The first half of this being unnecessarily precise, the second half, infuriatingly vague: "The fact is, I didn't want to place it in a specific time, or even a place. I said: 'Not only does it take place everywhere in the 20th century, but it takes place on the Los Angeles/Belfast border.'" [6]

Gilliam didn't want *Brazil* to fall into the trap in which *1984* found itself. He did not want its relevance to be pinned to a specific place or time, and therefore have it sidelined outside of that place and time.

The original plan was to feature visual cues from the entirety of the 20th century: Edwardian England in the restaurant scene, 20s art deco in Ida's house, German expressionism in the architecture of The Ministries, and so on. In practice, however, the film's design most consistently resembles America of the 40s and 50s. This was the period "...when we thought it was all going to get wonderful, that the American way was going to lead to a Utopia." [7]

One constant which runs like an umbilical through this film, connecting it directly to its predecessors, is Gilliam's fascination with exposing internal anatomy to the elements. Where this film lacks the decapitations of its forebears, and has almost none of the usual skeletons, it is wall-to-wall with intestinal imagery. To make his point more appropriate to his setting, Gilliam has distanced the grotesque biology from the characters, and instead filled their surroundings with it.

TVs and teletype machines have had the casings removed, so the guts can be seen. In the bustling, chaotic foyer of the Ministry, one of the film's few pieces of actual futuristic technology is a robot which, in common with all the other mechanical devices, has had its outer skin removed. This is far from just a casual interest or an aesthetic decision. This exposing of the workings of the machinery which surrounds his characters, relates directly to the human frailties of those characters: "I'm obsessed with viscera, whether mechanical or organic...the wiring, someone's intestines – they all seem the same to me." [8]

When Tuttle tears back the protective skin of Sam's walls to reveal the turmoil of pipes and ducts beyond, we hear the gurgling and rumbling of a great dyspeptic beast. "On one level, the world is totally inorganic, inhuman, yet, the minute you scrape away the surface, it's bleeding and throbbing and it's breathing like an animal..." [9]

Gilliam's fascination with ducts (which appear frequently in his Python animations) came from his first sightings of British stately homes, those great ancestral piles with impressive, elegant facades which, thanks to the march of progress, are now all defaced with elaborate mazes of external plumbing all, as Gilliam himself puts it, in the interests of "...getting rid of the shit."

In our society, the shit removal system is safely buried underground, where we never need think about it. In *Brazil*, the bowing, elasticated duct hanging ominously over your head, may well be the local sewer. This proximity to one's own outpourings, must have detrimental effects on some people's psyche; as demonstrated by the woman outside Information Retrieval, with the sticking plaster neatly applied to her poor little dog's backside.

Eventually, this concern forms the basis of one of the more memorable moments in the film: where Tuttle arranges death by sewage. "People talk in very proud, intellectual, academic terms about this film, and here we go, we just let people get stuck in the shit...there's nothing more fun than cheap, juvenile scatology." [10]

And, whilst we're on the subject of proud, intellectual academics: "...what Jean Baudrillard himself calls 'the unclean presence of everything'...is suggested most powerfully by the pulsing mass of *Alien*-like, quasi-organic, tentacular ducts and tubes which spill out into Sam Lowry's apartment" [11]. All of which makes the city seem like some huge slumbering beast. If this is so, then Sam and his fellow citizens crawl through the arteries and organs of this beast.

e notion of the workings behind the walls being alive, is also reflected in Information Retrieval where Sam's alleged father, Jeremiah, still supposedly lives within the fabric of the building. His name is immortalised as the anagram 'Ere I am JH' in Helpmann's elevator. He is, in other words, the ghost in the machine.

Strangely, until his walls are ripped away, Sam doesn't live like everyone else. He isn't constantly presented with the pipes and ducts. "Sam's got the purpose-built flat...you don't see the ungainly ducting sticking out of the place. This is smooth, everything's hidden behind the walls, like the world *we* live in, generally. Except, none of it works the way it's supposed to." [12]

This flat helps him in his denial of the way things are, because it hides the reality from his daily sight. Doubtless, he received this great privilege because of his mother's contacts, and therefore fails to appreciate just how comfortable his life is. I suspect the reason Central Services confound all expectations and actually turn up to repair his thermostat, also has a lot to do with Ida's contacts.

Inversions And Transformations: For the wealthy, bored and old of this society, transformation isn't so much a metaphorical concept as a way of life. Plastic surgery has made their meat eminently manipulable. In its depiction of this, *Brazil* uses transformation to deal with considerations of the grotesque *as well as* fantasy:

"Every time I come to Los Angeles, I pick up magazines in the hotel, and half of the pages are filled with ways of chopping and changing your body to be whatever you dream. It fascinates me. It's really, truly, an American disease...The mother's dreams are corrupted. They're immediate, short-term dreams about the now. They're not about anything really enriching, they're totally superficial." [13]

As Mrs Terrain is eaten away by her acid treatments, she becomes more fragile, more mortal. Tired, old, deluded and clearly dying from too much applied vanity, she waves a pair of crotchless panties at Sam and twitters "Imagine me in these!" This must be doubly distressing to Sam, given his sublimated desire for his mother.

Fantasies: Like Dennis Cooper before him, Sam Lowry is a man of limited aspirations, who has greatness unwillingly thrust upon him, when all he really wants is to lead a quiet, simple life.

However, Sam's fantasy life is very far from quiet and simple. He's got a full-on Freudian war going on in his unconscious: "Imagination might be defined as the ability to project something other than what is, in

44

such a way as to be able to realise the image in reality...Fantasy, as poor second choice, is the ghost of an imagination strangled." [14]

Sam had control in his little world in Records. His boss, Kurtzmann, being crippled by a mixture of indecision and guile, can't function without him. Sam saunters into work, several hours late, whistling, hat pushed back at a self-confidently jaunty angle. All the excitement in his life is consigned to his dreams, and there it would have stayed - had he not caught a glimpse of Jill on a CCTV monitor.

This brief non-encounter plants itself in the fertile soil of his imagination, and begins to spread. Slowly, incrementally, the passionate, adventurous life of his mind, begins to leak out into his humdrum existence. Motivated by an overwhelming desire to pursue this dream made flesh, Sam begins to deconstruct the safe, predictable world he had built for himself. One of the distinguishing characteristics of The System in which he and everyone he has ever met (except Tuttle) works, is that everybody maintains a studied ignorance of the moral consequences of their actions.

It is, therefore, not surprising that Sam, in jettisoning the life he has hitherto known, doesn't realise that he is burning his bridges and leaving himself terribly vulnerable to the unforgiving nature of The System. After leaving Records and entering the new and intimidating apparent efficiency of Information Retrieval, he is in a whole new, unpredictable world. At the same time, the mother he has known all his life is slipping away from him, transforming herself into something new and alien – a younger version of herself.

Increasingly, Sam relies on the reassuringly familiar narrative of his dreams but, even more increasingly, his doubts and fears about his real life, are reflected within those dreams. There is a progressive blurring of the line between fantasy and reality, with each impinging on the other.

Inspired by his desire for Jill (once he knows that she is real), Sam grows an ambitious streak. This, combined with his natural ability with computers, allows his real world situation and skill to bring a version of his dream world into being. Sounds ideal. Problem is, he doesn't cover his tracks with sufficient care. When he had access to Helpmann's computer, he should have used it to erase all of the mistakes and reportable incidents he had been involved in over the previous days. That would have ensured his future.

But Sam's failing has always been his naïveté, his willingness to believe that The System, despite its innumerable faults, essentially

. He can't possibly see the dangers of living in a world where no one thinks beyond the next piece of paper; because, his entire working life, he has been just the same. Because he is so ill-equipped to live in the real world, when his fantasy world collides with it, he has no idea how to cope. Unlike Harry Tuttle, who can function very adequately around the outskirts of The System, Sam is too domesticated, too restrained. But, it's not entirely his own fault:

Sam strains constantly under the yolk of his mother, who won't leave him be, and won't let him live his life as he chooses. Sam is very confused about his relationship with her, but she is also confused about her relationship to her own past. Sam's calm little insignificant life is disturbed by his mother's connections in high places, because she insists on moulding his life, in much the way Dr Jaffe will be moulding her face. Of course, our old friends the Freudians would say that given the absence of a father (Jeremiah is inexplicably long gone), Sam wouldn't want his mother to change and wouldn't want his own circumstances to change, but would rather maintain a form of status quo that he remembers from when his father *was* alive. Hence his distress at her plastic surgery, and at her insistence he should be promoted.

Further, he would want to subconsciously take the place of that father in his mother's life. We're edging, oh so tremulously, into Oedipal territory here.

When Jill finally submits to his affection, he takes her to his mother's house. There she dresses herself in his mother's sexy diaphanous silks, and one of his mother's wigs. Dressed like this, she becomes the vision from his dream. So, right there, on his mother's bed, with a woman wrapped in his mother's clothes, he indulges in what we are led to believe may very well be the first sex of his life.

Soon thereafter, during his final flight from the reality of torture, Sam sinks through layers of fantasy – firstly into the juvenile hero-fantasy of Tuttle's rescue and the big shoot-out. However, this fantasy goes sour, with his rescuer being literally consumed by the paperwork they thought they had defeated; after which, Sam moves into a second, darker level of fantasy – a nightmare.

He finds himself in a funeral, and there, surrounded by a crowd of suitors, sits his mother, wearing her idiomatic leopard-skin skirt and shoehat. Yet, when she turns to him, her plastic surgery now complete, she has become...Jill. A moment later, she has become his real mother once more, but the damage is done. Obviously his subconscious has been chewing over the similarities between Jill and Ida, and was beginning to generate some nice, healthy guilt over it. "Sam's condensation of Jill with his mother's regressive movement to her lost youth, tears the veil of Lowry's Oedipal secret: his Icarus dreams, grounded, are only so much infantile mother-lust." [15]

The shocking realisation that his uncontrolled passion for Jill has actually been him fulfilling his unconscious desire for his mother, consumes Sam and, as the Ministry Forces bear down on him, he plummets into the vaguely vaginal coffin (a literal depiction of the Oedipal motivation – which is a desire to return to the womb from whence one came). From here, he plummets into a recognisably Gilliamesque blackness, then emerges in the final layer of nightmare – the tenement alleyway, with the metaphorical Forces of Darkness mingling with the literal Forces of the Ministry, whilst he clambers over the refuse of spoiled lives, to escape. Suddenly, there is a door (another symbolic vagina), he plunges through it and finds himself safe in the womb-like interior of the domestic unit on the back of Jill's truck. This one-room dwelling will form their home, their security, their hideaway, as they head off into the happy ending he so desperately wishes for himself.

Here, in this stereotypical vision of domestic bliss, he can deny everything he learned about himself in his nightmares. At this point, he has sunk so deep into himself, Helpmann can, with complete justification, comment, "He's got away from us, Jack."

This notion of mother-lust is so distasteful, so unacceptable, that we automatically reject or ridicule it as an explanation of motivation. That's human nature. Maybe this is why Gilliam himself rejects this explanation of the funeral scene, and offers a rather limp alternative: "This isn't Jill becoming the mother. This is the mother becoming a very young girl who *just happens* to look like Jill. So, all of my Oedipus tendencies are not true!" [16] Yeah, and Pinocchio's a true story.

One way or another, Sam's juvenile, obsessive image of women, even the movie icons he decorates his bedroom walls with, will prove his downfall. When he finally meets Jill, he is shocked to find her in boots and leather jacket, driving a truck. Whilst visiting the hellish oil refinery, she picks up the mysterious parcel which turns out to be "bribes for official monkeys like you!" Jill is a survivor, determinedly independent and alone by choice: "You touched me. Nobody touches me." Yet, in order to make his power fantasy come true, Sam has to take her power and control away from her.

47

ft to her own devices, she would almost certainly have manoeu-vred her way out of trouble." [17] Yet, Sam's raging, infantile need won't let him leave her alone. By the end of the film, he has successfully taken her life away from her by officially 'killing' her, then he feminises her, moving her to peel off her defensive layers of clothing and re-dress her-self as his mother. To Sam, this has been his great act of heroism and finding Jill waiting for him in bed is his richly-earned hero's reward. "But the real Sam is incapable of resisting the secret police who smash in on them and the newly helpless Jill can only scream." [18]

Of course, I can't help but consider a slightly different view of these later scenes. After the death-by-sewage scene, Jill turns up on Sam's doorstep. How did she escape arrest at the lingerie shop, and how did she find Sam's house? Well, I'm glad you asked. It is my contention that this is one of the moments where the film actually deserves comparison to George Orwell's *1984*. Maybe whilst under arrest, Jill has been offered her freedom in return for setting up Sam. As Julia betrayed Winston Smith. Gilliam has insisted he had not read *1984* when he made *Brazil*. Whilst I have no doubt that is true, I find it unlikely that Tom Stoppard would also have missed it.

So, whilst Sam's short-sightedness has led to him leaving a massive catalogue of crimes in his wake, could it be that his naïveté and willing-ness to trust the friend all the posters insist he should be reporting, orchestrates his downfall?

Fantasy And Bureaucracy: Throughout the film, Sam's wish-fulfil-ment fantasies have been increasingly tainted by his fears and guilt about his activities in the real world. Indeed, they begin to percolate into his real life. Firstly he sees Jill in a dream, then on a computer monitor, then in a fragment of glass, then in her truck, before finally getting to meet her in person and finding that she is nothing like he expected.

Alternatively, the real world begins to impinge on his dreams in ever more persuasive ways. Initially, his fantasies are an idyllic vision of her-oism and chivalry, then the 'civilising' power of The System invades, as giant tenements are thrust out of the ground, effectively paving over the countryside he had been flying over. The skulking Forces of Darkness who are dragging Jill away represent that System, which is trying to keep her caged, and away from him. They wear baby-face masks because, throughout this society, everyone hides behind officialdom, protocol, and euphemism. Nothing is quite how it appears.

Glancing around a corner, he notices innocent bystanders, chained to the tenements, unable to escape, led by Mrs Buttle. These are the first stirrings of the guilt within him, but he ignores them and returns his attention to rescuing Jill. The ground rises up and forms itself into the bleating, needy form of Kurtzmann, reminding him of his promises not to leave, reminding him of the quiet, safe days when he didn't feel the need to fight The System.

But fight The System dream-Sam must. Yet, great pillars of brick, peopled by eerie lizard-like monsters are too surreal for him. He wants to be able to fight The System hand-to-hand, like in all those old movies which somehow get pumped into his office every day. So, he evokes a giant samurai.

Constructed of computer circuit boards, this figure gives The System an easily identifiable, and easily combatable, physical presence. Yes it is big but, like the mighty bronze giant Talos in *Jason and the Argonauts* (1963), it has a weakness which someone smaller, wittier and faster can exploit.

Unfortunately, when Sam bests the beast and removes its mask he sees his own horrified face gazing back. This is his subconscious pricking his guilt again, reminding him that he is actually part of this System he so wants to defeat. There is also the embarrassingly convenient semantic pun of the phrase "Sam, you are I," but we won't dwell on that.

Fred Glass' review of the film, seems to translate Gilliam's message as being a warning that the only way to elicit change is to avoid fantasising. Looking at the rest of the body of Gilliam's work, this cannot be so. I think it is far more likely that, as with *Time Bandits*, he is warning against using fantasy as a security blanket. He is encouraging us to explore the darker sides of our imagination in the hope that by doing so, we may, in some small part, inoculate ourselves against the darker sides of *real* life.

For Sam, the gap between his dreams and his ability to realise them, is an unbridgeable chasm, and this bitter, unacceptable truth, is contained within the film's title. The lyrics of the song *Brazil* evoke a utopian idyll. Of course, the word 'Utopia,' as coined by Sir Thomas More in 1516 to describe a perfect society, is taken from the Greek and literally means 'no place.' It is, by definition, a perfect society which *cannot* exist. So, the song, as first hummed by Tuttle, then picked up by Sam, indicates that the ideal to which they both aspire, is an impossible dream.

, then, is what happens when you slavishly follow your dream. Gilliam is asserting that relying romantically on fantasy, is a sure recipe for disaster. Fantasy is neither reliable, unimpeachable, nor the exclusive province of the special few. Throughout *Brazil*, he insinuates that *everyone* has wishes and dreams whether they be for youth, power or simply the chance to rebel. All the clerks in Sam's typing pool engage in a battle of wits with Kurtzmann by secretly watching the pirated movies on their monitors. Even the superlatively bland Harvey Lime, when he sees Jill's computer printout, suggests "Your dream-girl, is it!?" This implies that he, too, has dreams. And if him, why not everyone?!

The difference between everyone else and Sam is that he is consumed by his fantasies, whilst they restrict theirs to moments when dreaming won't detract from more important matters, such as staying out of the hands of Information Retrieval for another day.

Quotes:

1: Gilliam quoted on the audio commentary of the Criterion DVD of *Brazil*

2: Gilliam quoted in Kim 'Howard' Johnson, *Hello, Brazil*, *Starlog* 92, p55

3: Salman Rushdie, *The Location Of Brazil*, *American Film*, September 1985, p53

4: Gilliam quoted in Kim 'Howard' Johnson, *Life Before And After Python*, pp205-6

5: Gilliam quoted on the audio commentary of the Criterion DVD of *Brazil*

6: ibid

7: ibid

8: Gilliam quoted in Brian Howell, *Films And Filming*, March 1985

9: Gilliam quoted on the audio commentary of the Criterion DVD of *Brazil*

10: ibid

11: Fred Pfiel, *Another Tale To Tell*, p240

12: Gilliam quoted on the audio commentary of the Criterion DVD of *Brazil*

13: Fred Glass, *Film Quarterly*, Summer 1986, p25

14: Gilliam quoted on the audio commentary of the Criterion DVD of *Brazil*

15: Fred Glass, *Film Quarterly*, Summer 1986, pp24-5

16: Gilliam quoted on the audio commentary of the Criterion DVD of *Brazil*
17: John Hutton, *Nightmares Old And New, Jump Cut* 32, p7
18: ibid

The Adventures Of Baron Munchausen (1988)

"I always feel rejuvenated after a touch of adventure."

Cast: John Neville (Baron Munchausen), Sarah Polley (Sally Salt), Eric Idle (Desmond/Berthold), Charles McKeown (Rupert/Adolphus), Winston Dennis (Bill/Albrecht), Jack Purvis (Jeremy/Gustavus), Bill Paterson (Henry Salt), Valentina Cortese (Violet/Queen Ariadne), Uma Thurman (Rose/Venus), Alison Steadman (Daisy)

Cameos: Jonathan Pryce (Horatio Jackson), Ray Cooper (Functionary), Oliver Reed (Vulcan), Ray D Tutto [aka: Robin Williams] (King of the Moon), Sting (Heroic Officer)

Crew: Director: Gilliam, Writers: Charles McKeown & Gilliam, based on the novel by Rudolph Erich Raspe, Producers: Ray Cooper & Jake Eberts & Stratton Leopold & Thomas Schühly & David Tomblin, Music: Michael Kamen, Cinematographer: Giuseppe Rotunno, Production Design: Dante Ferretti, Make-up Design: Maggie Weston

The Plot: Somewhere in the 18th century, somewhere in Southern Europe, an unnamed walled city is being besieged by the forces of the Turkish army. Into the smoke and flames wanders an old man, who notices that the local theatre is presenting a play about the world's most famous liar: Baron Munchausen.

Well, since he himself is Baron Munchausen, he takes the stage and demands that the audience listen to 'the facts.' He insists that the war raging around the city started because of him, and only he can end it. Of course, no one believes the doddery old fool, except the theatre manager's young daughter who desperately wants to believe in magic and heroes.

Together they set off to find The Baron's gang – Berthold the swift, Adolphus the sure-shot, Albrecht the strong, and Gustavus who has super-strong breath. The search will take them from the city to The Moon, to the heart of a volcano and the gullet of a giant fish.

Despite the fact that his mission has taken decades off The Baron, all of his acolytes are old and disillusioned, talking fondly of the days when they were "...young and alive." So The Baron must reinspire his fellows, save the city and persuade one and all that this all really did happen.

The Thickening: The story behind this story is almost as fascinating as the story itself. Considerable coverage was given to the battle Gilliam endured getting the movie made, but the pedigree of the original book is, for me, just as fascinating.

Karl Friedrich Hieronymous von Munchausen of Bodenwereder was very much a real person. Born in Hanover in 1720, he served in the Russian cavalry in the campaigns against the Turks in 1740 and 1741. He eventually retired in glory in 1760. As was not uncommon in those days (and probably still isn't), this old warhorse made a new career for himself, telling greatly embroidered tales of his army years. So elaborate and fanciful were his tales that he very soon earned himself an international reputation. Which is where Munchausen's fellow Hanovarian, Rudolph Raspe (1739-94) enters the fray.

In 1769, Raspe became Professor at the Collegium Carolium in Cassel. Unfortunately, despite his intellectual gifts, Raspe was, at heart, a rogue. He couldn't resist the temptation of pawning much of the College's valuable collection of coins and jewels to supplement his not-insubstantial income. In 1775, the gaps in the collection were discovered and Raspe fled to Britain. It was here that he set to immortalising the tales of Baron Munchausen, a man he clearly felt an affinity towards although they had, in all likelihood, never met. The stories began to appear in 1781, and were gathered together in 1785 as *The Travels And Surprising Adventures Of Baron Munchausen* as allegedly written by the Baron. The following year a second edition appeared with further, even more fantastic tales. This edition was actually written by several hands, including the gothic poet Gottfried August Bürger (1747-94) although it, again, appeared under Munchausen's own name.

Thanks to 'his' books, the real Munchausen's reputation was destroyed, he became known as 'the world's greatest liar.' Then in 1798, one year after Munchausen's death, the news emerged that Bürger had actually written the tales. So it was, for many years, that the book was attributed to Bürger and both Raspe and the real Munchausen were forgotten.

The teller of tall tales had, as his legacy, become victim to people's inclination to believe complicated fiction in preference to simple truth. There may well be a lesson for Gilliam there.

Throughout 1987-88, Hollywood's news media delighted in detailing every problem Gilliam's massive production faced – a lot of which seems to have been motivated by Hollywood's glee at the departure of the first ever British studio head, David Puttnam, who had originally green-lighted *Munchausen*.

Still, many of the headaches and compromises that marked the production's infamy, were brought about by Gilliam's decision to shoot the film in Italy, with an almost entirely Italian crew. As producer Thomas Schühly explains, this decision was crucial to Gilliam realising his vision: "The English character, for me, is a very dark one...Italians are very light, very sensual...the film should get the feel of a very light atmosphere!" [1] Visually, it is certainly brighter than either *Time Bandits* or *Brazil*, benefiting from the glorious sunlight of its Spanish and Italian locations. I suspect that the film's initial critical mauling has a lot to do with the fact that it looks *too* bright and cheerful. You knew *Brazil* was an intelligent film with some serious subtext, because its predominantly blue and grey pallet gave it seeming gravity. *Munchausen* (with the exception of the sequence in the fish's belly) is all reds and sandy yellows. Certainly not the colours one expects to see in a meaningful movie!

Gilliam had difficulty explaining this to his Italian designers: "...who have this innate sense of beauty...it didn't *all* have to be beautiful - we could have crummy bits, visually quiet moments – but I never seemed to achieve that." [2] Then there was the tale's dubious associations with the Josef Von Baky's enormously expensive 1943 version, which Goebbels commissioned to use as fascist propaganda. The tale of a charismatic leader with the ability to lie convincingly to a gullible populace, clearly struck a chord in the Nazi High Command. Personally, I can't help but feel that anything that diverted vast quantities of money from building more tanks and bombs, is to be congratulated.

In point of fact, Gilliam's rendition of the tale, owes far more to Czech animator Karel Zeman's partly-live-action 1961 version *Baron Münchausen* (*Baron Prásil* as it is known in some countries). Zeman combined live action with puppetry and artificial, sometimes animated backdrops to produce a dreamy, surreal narrative. Zeman's style owes a very deliberate debt to that of cinema pioneer Georges Méliès, drawing heavily on *Journey Across The Impossible* (1904), and particularly on *Journey To The Moon* (1902) (that's the one with the face in The Moon, which Gilliam cheekily re-enacted at the beginning of his celebration of very early silent cinema, the TV series *The Last Machine*). Méliès employed the stagecraft of late 19th century theatre in his films, most obviously in his use of theatrical flats to create elaborate and fantastic sets. Zeman emulated this signature style for his film and, throughout his version of *Munchausen*, Gilliam also employs epic theatrical stagecraft.

This begins, as it did with *Time Bandits*, in a bomb-damaged theatre during a performance which Henry Salt insists "Holds a mirror up to nature!" The technique of employing moveable flats, weights, pulleys, ropes and giant props, certainly holds up a mirror to this film.

The tale The Baron tells, when he takes over the stage, also bears more than a passing resemblance to *Time Bandits*. It concerns taking a child on travels from ostensibly real locations such as the city, to fantastical locations such as Vulcan's forge, and deals throughout with the widening chasm that exists between the perception and the reality of heroism.

The Baron is a typical 18th century gentleman, with servants for whom he holds a healthy disregard. Although, on the surface, Berthold, Adolphus *et al* would appear to be equal partners in The Baron's adventures, the truth is they work for him. He has no real appreciation for their gifts, taking them as given and abusing them as a whim. He persistently shows greater affection to his horse than to them. This is first demonstrated when he rashly makes an impossible bet with The Sultan. Through teamwork, his servant's extraordinary abilities save his head from the chopping block, and subsequently clean out The Sultan's treasure house. After this, for reasons which are never explained, the gang splits up. The only hint as to what may have divided them, is given by Albrecht. His first reaction, upon seeing them after decades away, is to protest "I haven't got the treasure any more..."

Earlier, on The Moon, Berthold had been equally delighted to be reunited with The Baron: "I've been stuck here for over 20 years...You abandoned me here! You swine! You toddled off with the Queen of Tarts and left me to rot in that parrot cage."

In the original version of The Moon Sequence (the incredible vanishing budget necessitated substantial rewrites) there was to be a sub-plot about an eclipse. As the shadow of the eclipse passed across The Moon's surface, all those who were caught by it promptly lost their memories (hence Berthold not immediately remembering The Baron). However, The Baron needs no such stellar event to chase away his memory. Whenever he is presented with the spectre of a beautiful woman, he is entranced and his mission is lost in a beauty eclipse.

Throughout, his motivation (raising the siege and rescuing the city) keeps on being forgotten or ignored. Whenever Sally reminds him, he simply insists that the battle is over and the city is safe. Cue images of bombs exploding and city gates being rammed. It is fair to say that The

Baron survives on a diet of adoration and conceit. If other people don't think him wonderful, he despairs and ages. If, however, others admire him, he becomes younger and stronger and utterly full of self-regard. In reality, all of his adventures are about his need for constant reassurance, be it from Sally, his servants or any woman he comes across.

Seen in this light, his rescue from the clutches of Death, behind the theatre scenes, can be seen as something of a mixed blessing. He is brought back purely by the interest and willingness to listen of one inno- cent young girl. In other words, a fresh mind for him to corrupt with his lies.

Grotesquerie: One of Gilliam's stated aims when making *Mun- chausen*, was to bring to life the dark and broody illustrations Gustave Doré provided for the book. He decided to cast John Neville as The Baron, rather than the more famous Jonathan Pryce (who wanted the role) largely on the basis that Neville resembled Doré's depiction of The Baron. Also, Neville was a great and highly regarded actor (in the mould of Sir Ralph) who had somehow managed to stay on the stage and off the screen throughout most of his career; so he managed to be both famous and almost completely unknown at the same time – rather like the real Baron.

There are two moments where Gilliam most perfectly realises this dream, and both involve the cloaked, skeletal figure of Death: The first comes backstage at the theatre, when Death, complete with scythe and hourglass, is hunched over The Baron's prone figure, delicately drawing the life-force from his mouth. The tableau is lit by a typically Doréan beam of Heavenly light, and is otherwise shrouded in ominous shadow.

The second, equally dark moment, comes when The Baron and his gang investigate the belly of the great fish which has swallowed them, and find a landscape of wrecked, skeletal galleons. Apart from its Doré influence, this moment also draws on the legend of Jonah and his whale, as well as on *Pinocchio* (1940) one of Disney's earliest and most visu- ally baroque animated features which, along with *Thief Of Bagdad* (1940), was one of Gilliam's childhood favourites.

The 'Organ of Human Torture' is a very similar concept (if on a somewhat grander scale) to Python's *Mouse Organ*, with maybe just a dash of *Jabberwocky*'s human doorbell. The music The Sultan plays is called *The Torturer's Apprentice*: "Act Four is set in an abattoir. I see a lot of slapstick!"

All of this, combined with the Sultan's matter-of-fact approach to beheading, sits well with the source text's "...fondness for splitting or slicing bodies – commonly horses, dogs and diverse wild beasts." [3]

Indeed, the image which attracted Gilliam to the project in the first place (which, as with *Brazil*'s coal-blackened beach, never made it into the finished film) is one of the most famous of Doré's illustrations for Raspe's book: "...when [The Baron's] horse is cut in half by a portcullis and he's just riding on the front half of his horse – that was what I wanted to do more than anything. But we lost that before we started shooting." [4]

Nevertheless, there are still some impressively unnatural animals on display here. Ray, the King of The Moon, rides a giant three headed lunar turkey which splits into thirds, revealing the mechanical cogs and wheels beneath the skin. Likewise, Ray and Ariadne Moon are far less biological than they seem, being made of animated stone! Vulcan is also rendered non-bio for a moment, when his rage at seeing his wife with The Baron sends comedy steam whistling out of his ears. Later, The Baron leaves his own biological state behind and emulates Evil in *Time Bandits* by turning himself into a lethal carousel during the climactic battle with the Turks.

The ultimate taboo, from the perspective of observing the laws of nature, is the defiance of Death. Accordingly, The Baron's relationship with life and death is a remarkably inconsistent one. Horatio Jackson's refusal to believe in The Baron's "hot air and fantasy" strikes more of a mortal blow than his musket ball, because it is only doubt and criticism which wound Munchausen.

There is a very solemn burial, complete with epic Mozartian requiem, all of which is instantly deflated by the comment: "And that was only one of the several occasions on which I met my death!" His temporary death provides a perfect fairy-tale ending, again like *Time Bandits*', although, with a typically Gilliamesque proviso: "Everyone, who had a talent for it, lived happily ever after!"

Inversions And Transformations: In the film's opening moments, the benefits of heroism are turned on their head when an overly heroic soldier is executed because "This sort of behaviour is demoralising for the ordinary soldiers." Gilliam hasn't time for squeaky clean heroes, he likes his to have hidden agendas.

In a moment not dissimilar to the slave-ship shot in *The Crimson Permanent Assurance*, the gap between fantasy and reality is bridged by a simple camera pan, as the stage set of the Sultan's palace gives way to the real thing.

The voyage to the Moon reaches its conclusion through a clever shift in lighting, as a star field slowly transforms into a beach on which The Baron's gondola comes to rest.

When the jealous Ray/Roger realises that his wife is with the minuscule Baron, he roars "But you said size doesn't matter!" An amusing reversal of a very old lie!

In a sequence lifted almost bodily from *Time Bandits*, the gang are swirled around in a whirlpool, then float downward through water to the inverted surface – this transition is very like the journey from The Titanic to The Time of Legends.

Fantasies: And so, Gilliam got to complete his 'dreams' trilogy after all: "I just got more hooked on again my same old theme, Fantasy/Reality. Lies and truth is an extension of that...*Time Bandits* was a story about a boy going through space and time and history, and never knowing whether it was real or a dream; *Brazil* was about a man who refused to take his responsibility in the real world and spent his time dreaming, ultimately escaping in madness; and *Munchausen* is really the happy ending, the triumph of fantasy" [5]

The binary opposition which exists between The Baron and The Right Ordinary Horatio Jackson is best explained in their own words.

The Baron: "Your reality, sir, is lies and balderdash and I am delighted to say that I have no grasp of it whatsoever."

Jackson: "We cannot fly to The Moon, we cannot defy death. We must face the facts, not the folly of fantasists like you, who do not live in the real world."

The difference between their two positions is really one of faith. Jackson only believes that which is proven, The Baron survives on the belief of those who need no proof. As he ruefully points out, while they are rappelling off the point of the crescent Moon: "This is precisely the sort of thing that no one ever believes."

Be Headings: Of all Gilliam's films, *Munchausen* plays fastest and loosest with the human head. In the film's opening moments, we are given a tour of the war-torn town square, where a family huddles for shelter inside the hollow head of a decapitated statue. Later, during the ticker-tape parade, after the war is over, we see the statue being re-headed and learn that it is, in fact, of The Baron. This selfsame head which, in The Sultan's failure to remove it, was the cause of the whole war.

The separation of head from body, in a philosophical rather than literal sense, was one of the major concerns of René Descartes (1596-1650), whose work is now regarded as being one of the turning points in the Renaissance, as medievalism finally gave way to the Age of Reason – the very transition against which The Baron fights so persistently.

In 1637, against a backdrop of scientists being routinely condemned to death by the Catholic Inquisition for daring to hypothesise, Descartes published (anonymously, so that his own head and body might stay in touch) *Discourse On The Method*. He was debating whether or not we can prove that anything actually exists, or whether we are simply dreaming everything we do and are. His solution to this conundrum hinged on the most oft misquoted philosophical dictum there is: *"Je pense, donc je suis!"* No? Not ringing any bells? How about: *"Cogito ergo sum!"* It's on the tip of your tongue, isn't it! It is, of course: "I am thinking therefore I exist!"

What followed from this was the reduction of the human being into two distinct parts: the Res Cogitans ('Thinking thing' – the mind) and Res Extensa ('Extended thing' - the body). These are the two ingredients of what is now know as Cartesian Dualism which, in essence, insists that the body, the meat, is merely the vehicle which transports the mind around. The mind, he believed, could exist without the body because it does not exist in the physical, corporeal sense. Therefore, there was no reason for the body to be meat. It could be mechanical. It was the existence of the mind which made a person human, not the vehicle in which that mind resided. Upon his untimely death in Stockholm, Descartes' body was transported in state back to his home in France. Ironically (irony being the defining principle in many Gilliam films), along the way many devout relic hunters took to removing pieces of his body for worship. So, by the time he made it back to France, there wasn't much meat left.

Now, what has this to do with *Baron Munchausen*? Well, the film's consideration of Cartesian cranial concerns reaches a head on The Moon, where the personalities of The King and Queen are clearly divided between the needs of the body and the needs of the mind. As The Baron puts it, to an understandably incredulous Sally: "Their heads go off on intellectual pursuits while their bodies engage in more...bodily activities." Or, as The King himself puts it: "I, that is the head, where the brilliant and important parts are located, is now ruling the known universe. And that which I don't know, I create...'Cogito ergo es' – 'I think, therefore you is!'"

However, this separation between mind and body actually creates a situation where Ray (the head) is jealous of Roger's (the body) attentions to his wife. When head and body are reconnected, the higher functions are lost entirely and all the body wants to do is cram food into the mouth. The head's response: "I haven't got time for flatulence and orgasms!"

Bureaucracies: Horatio Jackson is the exact opposite of Sam Lowry (yet looks strangely like him, don't you think?) In the name of cold, hard and, it must be said, extremely childish rationalism, he is deliberately elongating the war with The Sultan: "The Sultan's demands are still not sufficiently rational. The only lasting peace is one based on reason and scientific principle." So, he could end it immediately, if only he wasn't sticking to the letter of his own deranged rules.

On the battlements, Sally discovers that the city's soldiers won't fight back, despite the terrible bombardment, because "It's Wednesday!" Presumably they bomb each other on alternate days, according to a rota.

Later, it transpires that Jackson has no real interest in "lasting peace" anyway. He is arranging a surrender, to take place "Three weeks from today," presumably booked so far in advance because he wants to keep his paperwork in order. But, of course, because they don't have it in writing, he and The Sultan cannot agree on who is to surrender: "We surrendered last time...so now it's your turn." Implying that any peace they achieve will be extremely short-lived, before they engage in a rematch.

Quotes:
1: Thomas Schühly quoted in David Morgan, *The Mad Adventures Of Terry Gilliam, Sight And Sound*, Autumn 1988, p239
2: Gilliam quoted in Ian Christie, *Gilliam On Gilliam*, pp183-4
3: David Morgan, *The Mad Adventures Of Terry Gilliam, Sight And Sound*, Autumn 1988, p240
4: Ian Penman, *Monster Munch, The Face*, Feb 1989, p100
5: David Morgan, *The Mad Adventures Of Terry Gilliam, Sight And Sound*, Autumn 1988, p240

Part Three: Renaissance Man

The Fisher King (1991)

"For-giiiive me!"

Cast: Jeff Bridges (Jack Lucas), Robin Williams (Parry), Mercedes Ruehl (Anne Napolitano), Amanda Plummer (Lydia Sinclair), Michael Jeter (Gay Bum), David Hyde Pierce (Lou Rosen), Christian Clemenson (Edwin), Kathy Najimy (Crazed Video Customer), Chris Howell (Red Knight), Lisa Blades (Parry's Wife)

Cameos: Harry Shearer (*On The Radio* Actor Ben Starr), Richard LaGravenese (Strait Jacket Yuppie), Tom Waits (Sid), John de Lancie (TV Executive), Mel Bourne (Langdon Carmichael)

Crew: Director: Gilliam, Writer: Richard LaGravenese, Producers: Debra Hill & Tony Mark & Lynda Obst & Stacey Sher, Music: George Fenton, Cinematographer: Roger Pratt, Editor: Lesley Walker

The Plot: Jack Lucas is an arrogant, offensive breakfast-show jock. He lives a spiritually empty life of moderate fame and riches, all of which comes crashing down when Edwin, the butt of one of his cruel on-air jokes, shoots up a restaurant full of yuppies.

Three years later, living in the back room of a video store, Jack is a suicidal alcoholic, determined to reject the love of Anne, who believes that all he needs is to accept that love. Standing beside a cardboard city, Jack decides to throw himself in the river and end it all but is rescued by Parry, an insane knight errant who believes he is on a quest to rescue all who are in despair, on his way to finding the Holy Grail.

Jack soon learns that Parry was once medieval historian Henry Sagan, who went mad when his wife was shot dead in front of him in the restaurant massacre. Seeing an opportunity to earn some kind of redemption, Jack determines to fix Parry up with Lydia, the woman he loves. And so, Parry and Jack are locked into a spiral where each can only achieve a healthy mental state, by rescuing the other.

The Thickening: The Fisher King was something of a rubicon for Gilliam. He signed up with a big American agent and began to receive scripts for his consideration. "Until *Fisher King*, Gilliam says he always felt the need to write the screenplay to make a film *his*." [1] However, so impressed was he with *The Fisher King*'s script, he wasted no time in breaking four of the non-negotiable rules he had lived his professional life by. He decided to work in America, to direct someone else's script, to sacrifice final cut and, most crushingly of all, *not* to cast an ex-Python.

Of course, it is not difficult to see why Gilliam would be attracted to this story: As he, himself, puts it: "There're still the elements of fantasy and reality, and madness and sanity, materialism and romance...they're all here. And there's definitely the search for the Holy Grail!" [2]

When we first meet Jack, he is shrouded in shadow, trapped in a dark, soulless cage. Not literally; rather it is a cage of his own personality. He is held in by a seemingly inexhaustible misanthropic rage and self-loathing which have trapped him into having to be offensive on cue. He is suffused with hatred - hatred for the media which feeds him, for the people who surround him, for the city in which he lives, but most of all, hatred for himself. His rant against the shallowness of yuppies is really his judgement of himself for being successful in this world he so despises. He is living his ego's dream, and he is deeply unhappy.

His studio walls are criss-crossed with bars of shadow. His home is a box of metal window frames, with nothing to offer comfort. Both rooms resemble cages. Jack is not a free man.

On the last night of the first act of his life's play, Jack languishes in the bath, in his ivory tower, rehearsing the catchphrase from the sitcom he is about to make: "For-giiiive me!" This is a phrase which will haunt him over the next few years, until finally he will realise that the only forgiveness he needs, is his own.

We are never told how he makes it from that sunken bathroom on the night of Edwin's massacre, to the back office of Anne's video store, three years later.

Anne is a fascinating character. Anne stands for everything that is real, everything that Jack (and Parry) are hiding from. She faces up to life and copes with it. It is not insignificant that she wears predominantly red clothing and make-up. As we shall see, red is the colour of Parry's fear but also, eventually, red will prove to be part of his and Jack's redemption. Much later, we will learn why red is such a key colour to Parry's delusions – why it forms the barrier between his old life and his new life. For now, we must merely take the red as read.

In some ways, Anne is the female equivalent of Parry. She is drawn to the dangerous and pained Jack because she knows that she can achieve happiness by offering it to him. For her, the Holy Grail is getting him to admit "I love you."

A child gazes up at Jack and, without comment, proffers a Pinocchio puppet. This silent symbol serves to illustrate that Jack feels like a marionette, no longer the man with 'The Power,' no longer master of his own destiny: "Ya ever get the feelin' sometimes...y'r bein' punished for y'r sins?" Of course, there is also the small matter that, rather like a particularly innocent wooden boy, he is in desperate need of a conscience

61

guide! "Anyone here named Jiminy?" He asks bitterly, as he stumbles off into the night...to meet his fate.

Soon he is discussing philosophy with his new wooden friend. It is entirely appropriate that the only philosopher a yuppie will have heard of at the end of the 80s, would be the fascists' poster-boy, Friedrich Nietzsche. The passage of his writings which has lodged in Jack's mind, concerns the belief that the people who weren't blessed with authority and good fortune were "the bungled and the botched." So comforted is he, by these words, that he is teetering on the banks of The Hudson, strapping breeze-blocks to his ankles; when the very next people he meets, put Nietzsche's caring old liberal philosophies into practice. Sick of seeing the bungled and the botched littering the streets of their upmarket neighbourhoods, a couple of bored, overly-privileged slacker kids pull up in their daddy's car, with the intention of improving the view with a can of petrol and a box of matches.

Enter Parry (né Henry Sagan), armed with a song, a smile and a self-made slingshot. He selflessly rescues Jack at the moment he had finally let go of his life. Now, after three years in Purgatory, Jack has finally abandoned himself to fate, and that fate brings him Parry, carried by a gust of dramatic irony (or divine intervention, depending on how you wanna look at it) ready to guide Jack through the mindfield to mental health.

When Jack learns that the life of Henry Sagan the historian ended in the yuppie restaurant massacre, he realises that, try as he might, he can't hide from his responsibilities: "I really feel like I'm cursed...I wish there was some way I could just pay the fine and go home."

In an attempt to make this happen, he strikes on the idea of giving Parry back some vestige of a normal life. He decides that his noble act must be to save Lydia from the jaws of the dragon of spinsterhood, and deliver her into the arms of Parry. Whilst an admirable and uncharacteristically altruistic effort, this succeeds in missing the point almost entirely.

Having succeeded in his selfishly-motivated mission, Jack feels sufficiently proud of himself to accept Anne's love. Next morning, however, all that remains of that good feeling is an erect ego. Jack has forgiven himself for his past crimes, he feels that his soul has been washed clean by his years in Purgatory and now he can begin living again. Unfortunately, with this acceptance, his arrogant old persona resurfaces.

But, as the doctor at the A&E reminds him: "The brain never loses anything – it just stores it up and waits. A person could actually re-experience the full effect of a tragedy long after the event took place." So, if Jack has grown a conscience, it can only be a matter of time before it comes back and gets him. Meanwhile, he is back in his studio, held in by its bars of shadow, the only colour in his world, other than grey, being the red of the LED lights.

Before Jack's reconversion, he needs to have that conscience pricked, by being reminded of the desperation he had witnessed during his time in Purgatory. This happens outside a great temple to Mammon (looking not greatly dissimilar to Donald Trump's eponymous sepulchre), which is emblazoned with a great '101' (and we all know what lies within room 101, don't we?) Once inside the tower, he is pitched a new sitcom: *Home Free*. It's a media executive's idea of homelessness, chirpy and upbeat and "...all about the joy of living!"

Suddenly, Jack realises that he has been once-again claimed by the Dark Side, that simply getting Parry to realise his love wasn't enough, that he hasn't paid the fine and he can't go home yet. At Parry's bedside, he rails: "This isn't over, is it!" In an attempt to rationalise, he complains: "I'm not God, I don't decide! I'm not responsible!" The ultimate denial, since responsibility is the thing from which he has been fleeing throughout the film. Then, finally, resignation: "No matter what I have, it feels like nothing." He leaves Parry the Pinocchio doll, the token which made Parry into Jack's conscience. One of his dismissive lines to Edwin, all those years before, was the simple, sarcastic: "Yeah, and Pinocchio's a true story!" Now, having plunged about as low as a person can go, he is rising to *make* Pinocchio a true story.

It is time for the King to act the fool.

The core of the film, and the key to its narrative, is the myth of The Fisher King, which Parry explains to Jack as they lay 'cloudbusting' in Central Park. The explanation in the script is far more detailed and far clearer, but it would have taken half an hour to tell. Essentially, the story concerns a young king, lost in a dark wood, who is presented with a vision of The Holy Grail. Knowing this to be a sure sign from God, the boy actually feels God-like in the presence of the Grail: "Innocent and foolish, he was blinded by greater visions – a life ahead filled with beauty and glory, hope and power... Tears filled his eyes as he sensed his own...invincibility." He reaches out to touch the Grail, to make his vision of his own glory become real, and his hands are burned by Holy fire.

Humiliated by this wound, he sinks into a depression, fuelled by his belief that he has lost the glorious future he saw for himself: "He became a bitter man. Life for him lost its reason. With each disappointment, with each betrayal, with each loss...this wound would grow...He lost the ability to love or be loved and he was so sick with experience...that he started to die." When many, many years later, a fool is brought to the court in an attempt to cheer the King, he simply sees an old man, in much pain, and asks what he can do to help. "I need a sip of water to cool my throat," croaks the King. So the fool picks a cup off the bedside table, fills it and proffers it to the king. Suddenly, inexplicably the king feels much better: "And then he looks to his hands and sees that it was the Holy Grail the fool handed him...an ordinary cup that had been beside his bed all along."

LaGravenese explains that the idea of translating this myth to a modern setting was given to him by "...a psychology book by Robert Johnson called *He*, in which the Fisher King, or Grail myth – when paralleled with the male psyche – becomes the story of every man's psychological and spiritual growth." [3]

Grotesquerie: In keeping with the ambience of the movie, the tearing open of bodies and revealing of their innards, is far less overt than in some of its predecessors. For example, Gilliam has found the most impressive city-block facades New York has to offer, and taken you behind them, to show the medieval squalor that the street people live in, just out of sight of Wall Street.

It is not insignificant that the first time we see 'the castle' of the Holy Grail, the foreground is dominated by a chimney belching fumes from the underground. New York may have built a concrete shield between itself and its inner workings, but they're still there, boiling and rumbling away.

This symbolic tearing back of the surface came naturally out of Gilliam's desire to honour LaGravenese's script, whilst also finding his own obsessions hidden within it. Throughout, Gilliam's dark view of medieval society percolates through the cold, stark modern exteriors. He eloquently makes the point that the excesses of grotesquerie which we laughed at in *Jabberwocky*, are still with us, and we can't put them down to a witty or ironic view of the past. Instead they are an uncompromising view of the present.

It is fitting that divinity and scatology should combine in the character of the displaced medieval knight, Parry – who not only refers to himself as "The janitor of God" (a role previously occupied by belligerent dwarves) he claims to have received his divine instruction when engaged in "...one of those really satisfying bowel movements, you know, the ones that border on mystical..."

He is the most Gilliamesque character here. He lives in a cluttered hole in the ground, lined with the outpourings of his imagination (as Kevin's bedroom was in *Time Bandits*) with a ceiling criss-crossed with pipes and ducts (as almost everywhere in *Brazil*). He is the torch-bearer, carrying the themes of existing Gilliam films forward into this new, altogether more modern incarnation.

The Gay Bum character, who isn't even dignified with a name, introduces Jack to a hellish world which exists in parallel to his own, a world he never suspected existed. The A&E he and Parry take Bum to, is a dirty, chaotic charnel house of derangement. Believing that he is looking at his own future, Jack takes an almost clinical interest in Gay Bum, politely enquiring: "Did you lose your mind all at once, or was it a slow, gradual process?" The answer introduces the idea of AIDS as the modern Black Plague, and also reinforces the all-too-easy-to-ignore idea that the suffering of the bungled and the botched is just as keen as the suffering of you or I: "I watched all my friends die...I sound like a veteran. Dad would be so proud!"

This point is then underlined by being immediately followed by the film's other key cameo: Tom Waits as Sid, the real veteran. He is begging for pennies and bitterly espousing his belief that he serves as "a moral traffic light" permanently turned to red, frightening people out of standing up for themselves. He is The 60s, crushed under the wheels of The 80s. He is the new reality – the reality of accepting that cage of conformity.

The significance of this character is ambiguous because, on the one hand, if Jack had known his place, and Edwin had known his place, then the tragedy would never have happened. On the other hand, bland acceptance of the way of things, leads to the system we see in *Brazil* and in Whitehall and on Capitol Hill.

Inversions And Transformations: I think it is an indisputable fact that *The Fisher King* features the best performances in a Gilliam film thus far. For the first time, the actors aren't competing against the unrestrained visuals, and so can explore their characters with greater depth than previous films have allowed. The moment when this becomes apparent, is when Jack's life comes crashing down around him, as illustrated by a penetrating, uncomfortably long close-up of Jeff Bridges' face, showing a deepening dread, an almost impossibly subtle tick at the corner of one eye being the one indication that somewhere in that mind, a personality has just collapsed.

Cut to a whole different world, and a whole different Jack. He skulks in the back room of a shop, which shivers in the shadow of the kind of glass and steel monolith in which he used to make his home. He is in the underworld, now. Obviously, one has to be brought low in order to rise again, and Jack will make many attempts to sink out of sight, once and for all, until he finally achieves his desire – and reaches the bottom.

When Parry sinks into coma, he and Jack swap places. Hitherto, Jack had been the wounded King and Parry the fool. Now, both having come some way down the path to health, they have swapped roles, and must continue in each other's shoes...or not at all. LaGravenese explains that this transformation is, for him, the whole point of the movie: "Parry becomes the wounded King and Jack must play the fool to steal the Grail that will save him. I hoped to convey that each man is both fool and wounded King. In other words, you don't need a Parry to find your higher self – he's already inside you." [4] And so it is that Jack finds himself dressed in Parry's rags, wearing Parry's hat and swinging from Parry's rope, as he climbs the outside of Langdon Carmichael's castle, wherein he will find The Grail.

Fantasies: Anne is the gatekeeper to a world of fantasy (the video store) but she is aware of the darker side of human needs, hence the reason she has all the porno videos in her office. In other words, she can balance the requirements of fantasy and reality.

Lydia's office similarly makes reality out of fantasy. Two Hearts Publishing sends out cheesy romance novels to people like Anne, in need of a fantasy fix. Yet, in reality, it is a corporation run from a cold and imposing high-rise block, and its offices are segregated by the same type of mini-partitions one finds in any sweatshop office, as well is in the labyrinth of Information Retrieval.

Although Parry is the delusional creation of a mind in hiding, the personality of Henry Sagan seeps through in subtle ways. For example, he knows that the redemption can only be achieved if he makes his peace with the man who orchestrated his tragedy. It is no accident that he and Jack should meet, as he all-but admits in his basement, when Jack first regains consciousness: "I'm Jack!" "I know!" It is entirely possible, given his tireless surveillance of Lydia, that Parry has employed the same approach with Jack, watching him and learning his habits before finally taking his chance to rescue him from the yuppies, and kick-start salvation.

Whilst attempting to liberate The Grail, Jack is faced with a stained-glass window bearing a red knight motif, and hears the sound of a horse. "Great, I'm hearing horses now. Parry will be so pleased." Inside, he continues to experience Parry's hallucinations - he imagines that Edwin awaits him, rifle loaded. Both he and Parry were casualties of Edwin's impotent rage, and now, finally, it is time for Jack to realise that, and forgive himself. After three years of suffering, he has paid the fine. Now, finally, he can collect his ticket and go home.

When Parry awakes, the tin cup he believes to be the Grail resting lightly in his hands, his first words are: "I had this dream, Jack..." Parry is gone now. He was only ever a dream, an alter ego, a knight defending Henry Sagan from a pain beyond bearing. But now, now that he knows there is still love in the world, and friendship, and honour; now that he knows it is a world he can still live in, Henry is back.

"I'm a singer by trade," Gay Bum confesses to Jack in the A&E. As he will later demonstrate, he is a singer of show tunes from musicals. The most fantastical of all Hollywood and Broadway genres. Originally rooted in ignoring the misery of The Great Depression, the musical is the last retreat of those who absolutely cannot cope with the bitter realities of life. In the video store, Lydia admits to liking musicals. Gay Bum only comes alive when he has a dress to wear and a song to sing: "I'm a man with a mission, Jack!"

The fantasy of the big musicals makes a brief reappearance in the film's closing moments, to celebrate Henry and Jack's return to health with a firework display. This demonstrates that, once cured, one can embrace fantasy again, and simply enjoy it for its escapism, rather than employing it as therapy.

Knights: Knights are a constant ingredient in a Gilliam film. In this film, the Red Knight is so integral to the fabric of the film, I can't ignore him.

Parry has a nemesis – the dreaded Red Knight. Up until the arrival of this spectre, the film has been a radical departure for Gilliam, far subtler and far more...normal, than anything previous. The smoke-shrouded, back-lit spectacle of the Red Knight drops us right slap in the middle of familiar Gilliam territory. Not only is this character a focus for Parry's medieval studies but its colour carries the mark of the reality that both he and Jack are hiding from.

The symbol of the knight and the therapeutic value of fantasy are intimately interwoven. Henry Sagan has immersed himself in his medieval fantasy, because he sees it as a time when salvation was possible – like the wounded Fisher King, he wants to be rescued, he wants to be sane. With this realisation, Parry sees a flash of red and The Knight appears in his peripheral vision, protecting him from the truth he cannot face.

In reality, Parry is constantly surrounded by red, be it garage doors, red-and-white pipes extending from manholes, or the red coat worn by the suicidal Gay Bum. His delusions insulate him from all this. The Jack-attacking yuppies drive a red car, yet he remains undaunted. At Anne's place, the phone is red, as is the sofa, as is much of Anne's wardrobe. Yet again, Parry is too distracted by thoughts of Lydia to be intimidated by this. However, when it comes to Langdon Carmichael's castle, resplendent in red brick, he cowers away. Later, when Jack is at his absolute lowest – listening to his tapes and using his newspaper cuttings to slash open old wounds - he is naked save for Anne's red silk robe. This is the reality *he* can't face.

It is only after Parry admits to loving Lydia and she employs the fateful phrase "You're real, aren't you" that we learn the true significance of the red to him. As her door closes on him, his reflection is divided, and for that brief moment both Parry and Henry Sagan stand side by side. "Please, let me have this..." he begs. The Red Knight storms down the road, attempting to rescue him from his reality once more, but it is too late. As he flees the knight, he runs through flashbacks to the night in the restaurant, to his wife, to his former self, to their happiness, to Edwin, to the shotgun and finally, most tellingly, to a vivid spray of red blood across his face as his wife's head is blown apart in front of him.

At that moment Henry sank into coma, eventually emerging as Parry; and red became the colour of reality...the colour he couldn't face. And with a trace of that happiness opening up all those old wounds, Parry also sinks into catatonia...possibly never to emerge.

When Jack breaks into Carmichael's castle, he stumbles upon the billionaire at the moment he is about to surrender his life, just as Jack was when Parry found him. Carmichael lies there in a red dressing gown, proving that, in reality, despair is the province of billionaires as much as beggars. With one simple act, Jack earns his symbolic red-emption and simultaneously cleans his own slate – he saves another man's life, by opening a door and breaking a laser beam which is, of course, red.

Quotes:
1: Johnson, Kim 'Howard', *The Real Fantasist. Starlog,* Spring 1994:
p68
2: Johnson, Kim 'Howard', *Life Before And After Monty Python,* p265
3: Richard LaGravenese, *The Fisher King: The Book Of The Film,* p124
4: ibid, p125

12 Monkeys (1995)

"They're asking for it. Maybe the human race deserves to be wiped out."

Cast: Bruce Willis (James Cole), Brad Pitt (Jeffrey Goines), Madeleine Stowe (Dr Kathryn Railly), Christopher Plummer (Dr Goines), David Morse (Dr Peters), Carol Florence (The Astrophysicist)

Cameos: Simon Jones (The Zoologist), Frank Gorshin (Dr Fletcher), Roger Pratt (Man Tying Shoe in Hotel)

Crew: Director: Gilliam, Writers: David Peoples & Janet Peoples, inspired by *La Jetée* by Chris Marker, Producers: A Veritable Football Team, Music: Paul Buckmaster & Charles Olins, Cinematographer: Roger Pratt, Editor: Mick Audsley

The Plot: By the end of 1996, five billion people died of an unnamed but highly contagious man-made virus. You probably read about it. By 2035, the one percent or so of us who survived, relocated underground. James Cole is volunteered to travel back in time to "...track the path of the virus."

Sent back to 1996, he actually overshoots and arrives in 1990, and is promptly arrested and thrown into an asylum, where he is the patient of the beautiful Dr Railly. Here he meets the hyperactive and utterly paranoid fellow patient, Jeffrey Goines.

On his second attempt, Cole successfully makes it to 1996, where he seeks out Railly, since she is the only person he knows, and forces her to help him trace The Army of the 12 Monkeys, the organisation he believes is responsible for releasing the virus.

It transpires that The Army is the brainchild of Goines, who seems to have taken Cole's 1990 predictions of Apocalypse to heart, and is determined to make them come to pass. So, is Cole indirectly responsible for destroying the human race? Can he help change the future? Or is he, in fact, imagining all of this?

In order to make this all a little clearer, I will be referring to the different time zones in the film, thusly: 2035 is 'the future/present,' 1996 is 'the present/past,' 1990 is, therefore 'the past present/past' and any time prior to that is, of course, 'the past/past.' There, simple.

The Thickening: 12 Monkeys is a complex spiral of ideas and concerns, all of which coil around each other in a fiendishly complex way. Co-written by David Peoples, who was also responsible for the equally labyrinthine *Blade Runner* (1982), the script makes incredibly dense reading – then Gilliam became involved and deepened and darkened it even further.

The title graphic is a mandala of slowly rotating monkeys. Mandalas generally symbolise the universe; this one symbolises this film, turning round and round in endless circles, with no clear beginning, no clear ending. The film itself begins and ends on a close-up of young Cole's eyes – gazing away into the future, or deep inside into his imagination?

In the opening moments of *12 Monkeys*, Gilliam seems to précis his career thus far: A dreamer wakes into an oppressive world where his wishes are ignored (*Time Bandits* and *Brazil*). He is given the chance to atone for past crimes (*Fisher King*) by saving the society which is under siege from an unseen enemy (*Jabberwocky*, *Brazil* and *Munchausen*). To do this he must immerse himself in barely functional technology (*Brazil*) and pass through a physical and metaphorical portal into the unknown beyond (all of the above).

The plastic suit he wears, and the caseless torch he carries, are both lifted straight from *Brazil*. The dilapidated power station he climbs up through, seems to hint at what Information Retrieval might look like after *Brazil*'s climactic bombing. Like the bandits, he has a map he must follow. Once away from the protection of the underground city, he finds the huge, grey stone monoliths of *Brazil* and *Fisher King* have become snow-white sepulchres. The world is now controlled by the huge vicious animals (lions, no tigers, but bears...oh my) which he has been selected to confront – as was Dennis in *Jabberwocky*.

As Cole rises from the underground, we are possibly even put in mind of Jack Lucas, who also had to rise from his tenure in Purgatory. Maybe this is Gilliam insisting that, with the success of *The Fisher King*, he has paid his dues over *Munchausen*...it's time to move on.

Even so, one can hardly call *12 Monkeys* a conformist movie. Gilliam may have, at least outwardly, been accepted as part of the Hollywood elite, but this hasn't persuaded him to bend to the will of the studios. He was determined to subvert the Hollywood system by making a big-budget movie, with high profile stars, and an intelligent script: "The public's expectations have been so lowered over the years...The films of the 40s and 50s wouldn't be made now, they're complex films and people would say 'Oh, it wouldn't work.'" [1]

Yet this is a very complex film. It weaves together two narrative strands – one concerning The Scientists of the future/present who are desperately trying to reclaim the future/future by piecing together their past/past. In much the way that Gilliam likes his films to become as an archaeological dig for the viewer, so The Scientists are scraping away the layers of time to reveal the few precious details which tell them the story of The Virus.

Meanwhile, 40 years previously...in the film's other narrative, Dr Railly also assembles the past/past through pictures and writings and deductive reasoning. Like The Scientists, she too has assembled a collage of pictures and articles and cuttings from which she draws inspiration for her theories.

Of course, Gilliam's distrust of scientists in general, and doctors in particular, remains undimmed. The Council of Scientists seem to run things underground yet they, like their counterparts in the present/past, don't actually take the risks themselves, they employ human lab rats like Cole for that. During Cole's 'interview,' they explain to him that they have sent back 'volunteers' before: "We've had some misfortunes with 'unstable' types." Cole will bump into some of these later.

Railly's lecture, 'Madness And Apocalyptic Visions' begins with a close-up view of the animated skeletons from Bruegel's *The Triumph Of Death* (1562). She discusses two peculiar cases, where prophets of doom have appeared in the past, and disappeared mysteriously. The second case employs the photo of Jose when in the trenches of WW1, researching the origins of Chemical Warfare. This implies that, if the second case were a time traveller, then the first may also have been: The woodcut of the medieval visitor (presumably researching the Black Plague) bears more than a passing resemblance to the ranting evangelist who will assail Cole in Philadelphia, yelling: "You're one of us, aren't you?" One can only suppose, he must have been one of the 'unstable types.'

So, the past/past is inextricably interwoven with the present/past and the future/present. Philadelphia, the location for the film's second half, was America's first capital. Now history has moved on. The asylum sequences were filmed in America's first penitentiary: "...and 'penitentiary' is a very specific word, it's about penitence, they weren't there to be punished, as such, they were there to discover their God." [2]

It is therefore appropriate that, now the focus of religious fervour has shifted from God to Man, so the purpose of this building should shift from penitence to psychiatry. In the present/past, such grand buildings, the kind which fill Renaissance paintings, are crumbling, graffitied shells. By 1996, late Capitalism has come to the end of its cycle, society is already dying. History is moving on.

My reading of the traditionally controversial Gilliam ending goes as follows: The big plan of The Scientists in the future/present, is to get Cole to locate The Virus, so that: "They'll send a Scientist back here, that Scientist will study The Virus then, when he goes back to the [future/] present, he and the rest of The Scientists will make a cure." It is, therefore, more than likely that Cole is being carefully scrutinised whilst fulfilling his mission. We know Jose is there, we also catch a glimpse of Cole's old Scarface guard. Both of these will make their reports to the future/present, and appropriate action will be taken. This is why The Female Astrophysicist is there on the plane, ready for Dr Peters. She is, as she freely admits, "...in insurance." Insuring against her world being forever subterranean. Possibly insuring against ours actually dying! Well, that's what I think.

Grotesquerie: Where your traditional Gilliam film delights in the grotesque exposure of the diseased and dirty innards of society, this one concentrates more on the paranoia associated with avoiding such exposures. Plastic and hygiene are the two most important ingredients in this. Yet, if orifices are the landscape of The Grotesque, the denizens of the future/present live in such orifices, deep beneath the calm, clean surface landscapes of the earth.

Cole is shaven bald, because hair is dirty. His entire life-story is contained in the bar-code tattooed on his neck. His secrets are laid bare for all (with a bar-code reader) to see. He is vulnerable, head bowed, posture submissive, voice lowered. He has no pride, no ego, no personal agenda, no personal possessions. He is (often literally) a naked man.

When he ventures up top, Cole has to encase himself in layers of rubber and plastic. This brings to mind the notion of a condom, as re-popularised in the 80s and 90s thanks to spread of the HIV virus. Beneath the transparent skin of the suit he wears, we can see the supportive straps and braces of the 'skeleton' and the tubes and pipes of 'lungs.' The naked man, fully clothed, is still exposed, still transparent.

When he comes back, he is interrogated by scientists who keep him restrained at a very safe distance, suspended halfway up a wall on an elevated chair, observing him through a robot bristling with cameras and television screens: "The video ball and the chair were important elements...when you're hanging up there; you're totally vulnerable. It's like a butterfly stuck on a wall, pinned down by scientists observing and dissecting it." [3]

These interrogators all wear plastic coats – Gilliam's shorthand for people one should distrust. The time machine is made of layers of plastic, encasing Cole in a bubble, an amniotic sac, from which he will be projected through a mechanical birth canal and be reborn in a whole new period. So, there is an undercurrent of life going on, even if it has been sterilised, wrapped in plastic and now exists only in a machinic form.

Throughout this film, there is an undercurrent of fear. People are frightened of other people, of either being attacked or infected by them. In the asylum games room, Goines assures Cole that, if inmates had access to telephones "...it could spread. Insanity oozing through telephone cables, oozing into the ears of all those poor sane people, infecting them! Whackos everywhere! A plague of madness..."

Much of what Goines sees is very sane, it's just his way of presenting it which frightens people: "My father is God! I worship my father!" Certainly his father, The Virologist, has the power of God. Which rather puts one in mind of Robert Oppenheimer's judgement upon himself and his A-bomb, when he paraphrased the *Bhagavad Gita*: "I am become Death, the destroyer of worlds." Much later, we are introduced to Dr Goines, the all powerful father, as he discusses the dangers of science: "...from Prometheus stealing fire from the Gods to the Cold War era of the *Dr. Strangelove* Terror...Never before...has science given us so much reason to fear the power we have at hand." As with Oppenheimer, he is not oblivious to the moral implications of what he does.

One of the key aspects of Grotesquerie, which is particularly appropriate here, is the wilful fragmenting of the normal progression of time. In a cheekily knowing line ad-libbed by Pitt, Jeffrey Goines insists: "But you can't turn back time, thank you Einstein."

Cole, however, completely fragments the concept of a time continuum – when he is in 1990, he refers to 1996 as the past, whilst 2035 isn't the future, it is the present. Railly, meanwhile, has "...the strangest feeling I've met you before...a long time ago, perhaps." Does she remember him as a child? Is she 'remembering' her future?

When they are together in their car, Cole gets all tearful over the 50s music the radio plays, yet this is the kind of music Bruce Willis would remember from *his* childhood. Cole was supposedly born in 1990. Or maybe he just went mad then.

Gilliam was attracted to this tale by the poetry of a man's entire life being haunted by the fact that he had, without consciously realising it, already witnessed his own death. This is touched upon in Railly's lecture when she discusses The Cassandra Complex: "Cassandra, in Greek legend you will recall, was condemned to know the future but to be disbelieved when she foretold it. Hence, the agony of foreknowledge combined with impotence to do anything about it."

There is, however, a far more corporeal form of agony afforded by time travel: when Jose is sent back to the 1914-18 war, he receives a deep facial scar which he takes back to the future/present with him. Scarface guard has, as his name may imply to the sharper reader, experienced similar disfigurement.

This, then, is the one similarity this film bears to Willis' other, more heroic roles - the amount of leaking he does. John McClane would always limp to the end of a *Die Hard* film dowsed in his own (and other people's) blood. Here, every time Cole leaves the future/present, he ends up bleeding or drooling or sweating. At one point he even finds himself crying. He just can't keep those nasty, horrible, disease-carrying bodily fluids in. So it seems there is a price to pay for defying Einstein.

Inversions And Transformations: For this film, Gilliam's casting decisions were, to some extent, the reverse of what would have been expected. Willis was used to playing the proactive action man, yet here he is cowed and quiet and very, very still. Pitt had developed a reputation for playing laid-back, slothful characters and here he is hyperactive. "What was so interesting was that Pitt was so determined to prove that he could do it; and, in a sense, that was true of Bruce as well. These are people who are trying to show to the world that they have a greater range than The System encourages." [4] So they conspired in Gilliam's desire to subvert and invert people's expectations.

In the asylum day room, the television in a cage shows images of animals in cages, being tortured by vivisectionists. The viewers are also trapped in a huge cage. By 2035, all humans will live in cages, like animals, whilst the real animals will roam the surface world freely...as nature intended.

"Monkeys, we're all monkeys!" Yells Goines at the TV. To underline this, it goes on to show The Marx Bros movie *Monkey Business*. Later, during a commercial break, animals are seen morphing into other animals, transforming thanks to the wonders of modern science.

When Cole escapes the cage, he notices that the security guard, who momentarily transforms into Scarface guard, is reading *The Enquirer*, which has a picture of a 'bat child' on the front page. Cole is being constantly bombarded by media images of animals and people in transformation. Throughout, he is exposed to images of caged animals, either in zoos or, more worryingly, in laboratories. We are increasingly invited to see Cole as an animal caged, like Goines. Which goes some way to explaining the motives behind the notion Goines will eventually have, of The Army of the 12 Monkeys.

Fantasies: This film's approach to the perennial Gilliam question of the relationship reality has to fantasy, is summed up by TJ Washington: "I don't really come from outer space...it's a condition of mental divergence. I found myself on the planet Ogo...I am mentally divergent in that I am escaping certain unnamed realities that plague my life here. When I stop going there, I will be well."

Since this description is certainly true of so many Gilliam characters, it nicely plants the seed of an idea in the minds of both the viewer and Cole – the thought that maybe he is hallucinating. Previously, it has been fairly obvious when a Gilliam character was dreaming, and when not. Here, the entire film could be a hallucination...or not. But, even if we accept that it is, we still don't know whether Cole is hallucinating in an asylum in the past present/past, or in his cage in the future/present.

The mysterious 'Bob' voice Cole hears when he is alone, could well be in his head. However, the bum he bumps into outside The Army of the 12 Monkeys office, the source of that voice could be another volunteer. Teasingly, the voice offers some suggestions, just to add to Cole's confusion: "Maybe I'm in the next cell, another volunteer like you....Or, hey, maybe I'm not even here; maybe I'm just in your head. No way to confirm anything."

Out in the woods, Railly, whilst whacking Cole over the head for imprisoning her in the boot of the car, is explaining to him: "You've created something in your mind, James: A substitute reality. In order to avoid something you don't want to face." She later refers to this as: "...a meticulously constructed fantasy world, and that world is starting to disintegrate. He needs help." Cole, now desperate not to believe he is responsible for destroying mankind, is clutching at any available straw: "I'm 'mentally divergent'; I would love to believe that!"

Of course, since a heart of irony lies beneath the surface of most Gilliam films, it is at precisely this moment that Railly begins to believe

Cole. Everyone else patiently points out to her that this could well be a side effect of the extreme stress she has been under, but she roundly rejects any psychoanalytical answer: "Psychiatry, it's the latest religion and we're the priests. We decide what's right and what's wrong. We decide who's crazy and who's not. Well, I'm in trouble here. I'm losing my faith."

Progressively, the ingredients of Cole's possible hallucination are re-presented to him in his real-life experiences. When he is on the run in the asylum, he stumbles upon the CAT Scanner, a hole in a wall which resembles the time machine. Soon after this, Cole begins to find the details from the future/present appearing in the present/past, rather than the other way round: He sees a photograph of Railly's graffiti before he sees her write it, he also hears the tape of her answerphone message, before he hears her make it. Most tellingly, he finds himself walking around the same streets he walked (under very different circumstances) during the film's opening moments.

If we are to accept the Cole-is-balmy hypothesis, this change must have come about because the onus is now on the future/present to prove itself real, since he is losing faith in it.

"You know what is real now?" He is asked. "Yes sir, I do." This is the first lie he has told The Scientists. He previously had no motive to deceive, but now he wants desperately to return to the fresh air, to Railly, and to the possibility of saving the world. To counter that, all The Scientists have to offer is a full pardon and freedom but, since we have seen nothing of the underground world save its prison and laboratories, we have no idea how much of an enticement this constitutes. I'm guessing: Not much.

Which reality would you choose?

Quotes:

1: Gilliam quoted on the audio commentary to the Region 1 DVD of *12 Monkeys*

2: ibid

3: ibid

4: ibid

5: ibid

Fear And Loathing In Las Vegas (1998)

"No Sympathy for The Devil."

Cast: Johnny Depp (Raoul Duke), Benicio Del Toro (Dr Gonzo)

Cameos: Katherine Helmond (Reservations Clerk), Christina Ricci (Lucy), Michael Jeter (L Ron Bumquist), Ellen Barkin (Waitress), Mark Harmon (Magazine Reporter), Cameron Diaz (TV Reporter), Tim Thomerson (Hoodlum), Debbie Reynolds (Debbie Reynolds' Voice), Lyle Lovett (Road Person), Flea (Musician), Gary Busey (Highway Patrolman), Harry Dean Stanton (Judge), Jenette Goldstein (Alice the Maid), Penn Gillette (Carnie), Hunter S Thompson (Old Raoul Duke), Ray Cooper (Distinguished Man in *The Dress Pattern*)

Crew: Director: Gilliam, Writers: Gilliam & Tony Grisoni and Tod Davies & Alex Cox, based on the book by Hunter S Thompson, Producers: Another Bloody Great Crowd, Music: Ray Cooper & Michael Kamen, Cinematographer: Nicola Pecorini, Editor: Lesley Walker, Demon Make-up Effects: Rob Bottin

The (For Want Of A More Accurate Term) Plot: Raoul Duke is a journalist (not entirely unlike his creator Hunter S Thompson) who, in the anarchic days of 1971, is ordered to go to Las Vegas to cover the Mint 400 cross-desert race. He elects to take with him his illustrious Samoan lawyer, Dr Gonzo. This isn't his first mistake.

In the depressing days after the Love Generation failed to make peace not war, Duke and Gonzo are no strangers to the pills and potions of the world's chemists. So they arrive in Las Vegas utterly stoned.

We follow them around, as they stumble through nightmare fantasies, with occasional detours into nightmare realities. As Duke's fear and paranoia increase, Gonzo wilfully drags him ever deeper into derangement, depravity and violence. All in the name of journalism.

The Thickening: Making *Fear And Loathing* was clearly a liberating experience for Gilliam. It has the drive and irreverence of a movie made by a film-maker in his early 20s, not his late 50s, coming closer than any of his other films to approximating the spirit of the original Python TV shows. Late Python, that is. The darker, less familiar stuff which the BBC rarely re-shows and which Gilliam has admitted contains some of his favourite Python material.

Fear And Loathing is dangerous, anarchic, and occasionally very frightening. It has a fractured narrative, with sudden bursts of extreme surrealism, all held together by central characters who are constantly changing. It commemorates "the brutish realities of this foul year of our Lord, 1971" by articulating Hunter S Thompson's memories and combining them with Gilliam's.

"It was the movie that brought [Gilliam] back not only to his home country, but to the era and the sentiment that had led to his self-imposed exile...If the American Dream was dead, then surely it should be the mad people – the Thompsons, the Gilliams – that got to dance on its grave" [1]

Since Gilliam routinely spends years writing and rewriting scripts, with any number of collaborators, the manner in which the *Fear And Loathing* script came about pretty much set the tone for the whole production process and, indeed, for the film itself.

"So [Tony Grisoni and I] sat down at my computer and wrote a script in eight days. Then we read what we thought was a great script, realised it was crap and rewrote it in two days. You feel a heavy responsibility doing a book that was such a seminal work – and by a living writer who carries a gun!" [2]

The resulting script had only limited success in lending a linear narrative form to Thompson's meanderings. It also betrays its hasty composition and this, I suspect, is why much of the finished film's spoken dialogue is ad-libbed or embroidered around the scripted dialogue.

Del Toro's speech is as slurred and garbled as it was in *The Usual Suspects* (1995), and both he and Duke rattle through their barely-discernible lines at machine-gun pace. The one time Duke needs to communicate clearly with Gonzo – when the suicidal paranoiac is threatening both their lives and needs talking out of it – he uses a loud hailer. Mostly, though, I had to sit with script open in front of me to follow their discussions. Which is where Depp's ad-libbing proved really helpful.

Duke and Gonzo are characters perpetually in a state of desperation, and the cause is sadly simple: With the Summer of Love a distant memory, the beautiful people had to face up to the realisation that the Counter Culture didn't count at all: "[In 1968] we were riding the crest of a high and beautiful wave...with the right kind of eyes you can almost see the high water mark – that place where the wave finally broke and rolled back." The survivors of that Acid Wave are now stranded on the beach, like crabs, scuttling around, out of their element...lost, frightened and unable to cope.

As he drives out of town, Duke passes the sun-bleached skeletons of those not fortunate enough to have escaped Vegas, and refers to the Love Generation (symbolised, now, by these bones) as: "...a generation of permanent cripples, failed seekers, who never understood the essential old-mystic fallacy of the Acid Culture: the desperate assumption that somebody...or at least some force – is tending the light at the end of the tunnel."

Fear And Loathing projects a very old-testament vision of Vegas, of a moral darkness beneath the showbiz glitter: "...It's like Bad Boy's Island in *Pinocchio*: it's beautiful and it's got everything, yet there's a rot at the centre which is actually destroying something." [3]

When he goes and mingles with supposedly normal people, Duke finds a strange affinity with them, as they sweat and suffer, unable to leave the gaming tables even at 4.30 in the morning: "Still humping the American Dream, that vision of the big winner somehow emerging from the last-minute pre-dawn chaos." Their desperation is similar to his. His key to blending in with these people: "Learn to enjoy losing." Although his engorged ego will never allow him to actually enjoy losing, he garners a lot of solace from actually being lost!

Duke's paranoia looks out at the state the world is in; but Gonzo's is more narcissistic, fuelled by his raging end-of-the-90s-style messiah complex. When Duke burst in on the bad doctor and his teenage victim, Lucy, Gonzo is very deliberately dressed as Jesus. He has corrupted the girl with drugs and then, it is implied, raped her. After Duke explains, in the starkest possible terms, the ramifications of this liaison with a minor in a hotel full of police officers, Gonzo bleats: "They'll crucify me." And wouldn't that be a shame.

If there is a corrupt heart of the America seen here, Gonzo is it. He leads Duke through various strata of America's Gomorrah – from casino to casino and from hallucination to hallucination - like Virgil leading the Christian through Hell in Dante's *Inferno*. When Duke decides he must escape, it is from the compromising situation Gonzo has left him in. As he roars down the desert highway, praying to God to be allowed out, demons appear to block his way – first the eerie hitchhiker, then the Highway Patrolman (an unavoidable nod to Alex Cox's 1991 film of the same name). "Oh, you evil bastard" He tells God – an oath an older, sourer Kevin Lotterby might join him in. Unfortunately, Duke is completely in Gonzo's thrall, even over the phone, so when he is told to return to Vegas, he finds himself complying.

We begin to understand just how demonic Gonzo is during the scene in the elevator. In the script, this is merely embarrassing as he turns his attentions to the female reporter. In the film, with the introduction of his ubiquitous hunting knife, the moment becomes truly terrifying. Gonzo is pure raging ego, wildly brandishing his knife, the symbol of his machismo, his sexual tool. When the waitress he propositions has the temerity to strike back at him, his normally manic manner becomes very, very still. This is worryingly uncommon, and makes him seem all the more chillingly dangerous. Duke's solemn reaction is the first naturally-lit, non-wide-angled close-up we have had of him. This is the first time we see him as anything other than a caricature, a cartoon figure. Suddenly he is very, very sober.

When Gonzo produces his hunting knife once more, and bears down on the waitress with it, it isn't surreal, it isn't hyperreal, it is all too chillingly real. The only other touches of real these close-ups have shown us is by inference – in the trickle of dried blood emanating from Duke's ear, or the vacant expression on Lucy's face when they stumble across her again. Gilliam brings us in close to see the reality of the damage this extended binge has done. When he wants us to see the binge in process, he pulls back, screws on a wide-angle lens and lets us take it *all* in.

In the final scene, retained in the script but cut from the film, Duke meets decent Norman Rockwell-type folk and his inherent cynicism offends them. Finally, after all he has done, he feels ashamed of himself so takes some amyl and forgives himself. How curiously Catholic.

Duke's one redeeming feature is that he knows he is shallow. He simply *can't* change, he's too weak. Maybe Thompson's book was an attempt at redeeming himself - not through amyl, but through confession: "You are now leaving Fear And Loathing: Population Zero!"

Of course, in a career path pitted with the craters of wars with The Studios, the battle Gilliam ended up fighting over *Fear And Loathing* was the most unusual of his career. He found himself fighting to have himself recognised as the writer of his own script since such matters are not, as one may assume, self-evident, but entirely decided at the behest of a trade union: The Writers' Guild.

The problem arose because British ex-pat Alex Cox had originally been scheduled to direct the film from a script he wrote with Tod Davies. His approach to adapting the book was radically different to Gilliam's, which is why Gilliam and Grisoni rewrote the script, which, in turn, is why The Guild got confused.

As Cox insists: "I started out wanting to have the pterodactyls, iguanas and so on, but the longer I worked on the script, the more interested I became in what the book had to say about the political situation...Personally, I don't think you need to show the bats and reptiles, you just need to give the impression that they exist in Duke and Gonzo's addled minds." [4]

This, then, forms the crux of the difference between Cox's and Gilliam's respective approaches to the film. The conundrum The Guild seemed to have such trouble with, was in working out how much Gilliam's script owed to Cox's, and how much directly to Thompson's book.

David Morgan, in his excellent website *Wide Angle/Closeup*, compares the Cox/Davies and Gilliam/Grisoni scripts to each other, and to the original book, in exacting detail. Ultimately, he concludes: "If Cox's script had never existed, or had never been read by Gilliam, the subsequent Gilliam script would be little different than the present one ..." [5]

So, infuriated at his inability to get sense from The Guild to which he paid a not-insubstantial percentage of his wages, Gilliam shot a very brief short entitled *The Dress Pattern*, where Ray Cooper asserts that the film wasn't made from a script, but actually from - you guessed it – a dress pattern. This text was eventually to see the light of day as the introduction of the published screenplay.

Ultimately, The Guild compromised and generously allowed Gilliam and Grisoni to be credited along with Cox and Davies. *The Dress Pattern* didn't play with *Fear And Loathing* (expect it to turn up on a DVD special edition, one day). Nevertheless, the damage was done. Gilliam publicly burned his Writers' Guild membership card – finally putting into practice a contempt for Guilds he has held for at least as far back as *Jabberwocky*!

Grotesquerie: At Bazooko's there is a high-wire act featuring a woman giving birth at high altitude. Another makes literal Thompson's description of 'nymphettes and wolverines.' Otherwise, Bazooko's is ringed by warped mirrors which create distorted, morphed reflections. It is a pandemonium of dwarves and giants and mutants which genuinely chills Duke: "A drug person can learn to cope with things like seeing their dead grandmother crawling up their leg with a knife in her teeth, but nobody should be asked to handle this trip."

As he flees Vegas, he passes animal skeletons projecting from the arid ground – a visual reminder of almost every Gilliam film I have discussed.

The weird hitch-hiker Duke encounters when attempting to escape Vegas, wears a T-shirt bearing Steadman's gruesome rendition of Mickey Mouse. This combines the two sides of Las Vegas in one handy image - the children's playground of the modern, with the dark seedy underbelly of the old.

Inversions And Transformations: When Duke arrives in Las Vegas, the effects of the acid he has dropped build – a car-park attendant's face warps slightly, then the carpets begin to crawl, and finally the desk clerk's head transforms into an eel. She is played by Katherine Helmond, so she is not unaccustomed to Gilliam transforming her face into something monstrous!

At the bar, Duke finds the patron sitting beside him has become a lizard, just as William Lee found a Mugwump sitting beside him during his visit to the fictional city of Interzone in David Cronenberg's adaptation of William Burrough's *The Naked Lunch*.

These morphed mutations, beginning with the one of Johnny Depp's face which adorns the film's poster and video sleeve have, with the aid of the computer, finally given Gilliam the ability to stretch and manipulate the very flesh of his actors. As one commentator has noted: "Python often did its best to turn the company themselves into cartoon, and this persists in Gilliam's films, where the director routinely regards his actors as objects to be bent out of shape, to be puttied and catapulted, folded and flung at will." [6]

Gonzo seems to look positively upon this, when he discusses the ravages of consuming *extreme* drugs: "Your body would turn to wax...they'd have to put you in a wheelbarrow."

Forced to be constantly vigilant of Gonzo's violent mood swings, Duke notes: "One of the things you learn, after years of dealing with drug people, is that you can turn your back on a person, but never turn your back on a drug. Especially when it's waving a razor-sharp hunting knife in your eye." So Duke is alleging that, under the influence of the drug, the person is lost and actually *becomes* the drug. Depp's single most impressive acting moment, comes when he *becomes* the industrial-strength hallucinogenic Adrenochrome. In the longest sustained take of the film, Depp acts his socks off, transforming right there, in extreme close-up, without the aid of make-up or special effects, from a confused, timid, reasonably coherent degenerate, into a creature several steps further down the food chain.

Under this influence, Duke sees Gonzo transform into a demon with horns (possibly his true form?) As he is changing, he is discussing the transformative power of eating "...extract of pineal...[you] grow horns...bleeding warts...then you'll notice about six huge hairy tits swelling up on your back!" A real Chimeric mutation of classic proportions!

Fantasies: In the film's opening moments, Duke hallucinates bats, guarding the entrance to Las Vegas, warning of the doom to come? As he drives away, one of these unreal bats is left crushed on the road. So, immediately, the fabric which separates dream from reality has been torn. In *Time Bandits*, Kevin's odyssey came to a close with this trademark Gilliam motif, when he discovered the photos which had no earthly right to exist. Duke's journey begins with that same realisation.

This film, more than in any of its predecessors, looks long and hard at the realities of living a life of fantasy. Spending your time stoned into denial is most unambiguously *not* a healthy life choice. These fantasies are not natural, they are not diagnostic, they are chemical fantasies which confound rather than assist mental health.

"In this Dantesque rendition of the American Dream, which recalls Hieronymus Bosch and Lewis Carroll by turns, the doors of perception open to reveal not a magical Oz peopled by the beautiful, but a spiky underworld of corruption ..." [7]

The Jefferson Airplane music Gonzo wants to die to actually projects Duke back into a flashback to 1965 and The Great San Francisco Acid Wave where he sees an older version of himself (played, of course, by his progenitor – Hunter S Thompson) in the third person. "Oh my God. There I was." Later, he receives a telegram from Gonzo, addressed to him under the pseudonym Thompson. So, the common ground between Gilliam and Thompson's interests seems to be where the boundary between the real and the imagined is worn away.

Since I have persistently violated my promise not to rely on quotes from Gilliam throughout this book, I feel it only right to conclude my analysis (if such it can be termed) with one. One which, to me, sums up the ongoing work of Terry Gilliam, and the lessons I learned while writing this book, and maybe offers a respectful word of advice to those who swiftly dismiss Gilliam's films after a single viewing: "At least Duke learns something...but have I learned anything? I'm still trying to work out: wisdom takes longer than it takes to see a film." [8]

Quotes:
1: McCabe, *Dark Knights And Holy Fools*, p175
2: Gilliam quoted in Ian Christie, *Gilliam On Gilliam*, p24
3: ibid, p260
4: Alex Cox quoted from an unpublished interview with Richard Luck, April 1998
5: David Morgan, *Fear Under The Microscope*, from his website *Wide Angle/Closeup*
6: Ian Penman, *Monster Munch*, *The Face*, Feb 1989, p98
7: Linda Ruth Williams, *Review*, *Sight And Sound*, Nov 1998, p49
8: Gilliam quoted in Ian Christie, *Gilliam On Gilliam*, p264

Outroduction: Gilliam's Unfilmography

"The movie never changes, it can't change, but every time you see it, it seems to be different because you're different. You notice different things."

- *James Cole, discussing Hitchcock's* Vertigo, 1996 (?)

In closing, then, it just remains for me to remark, belatedly I'll admit, that all of the insubstantial opinions and theories with which I have filled these pages, are simply that. While careful viewing of a film, any film, will doubtless throw up evidence which seemingly supports one reading of it, or another, it is not for us to say which reading is actually *right*.

Gilliam's films are delightfully (and frustratingly) mercurial. Where his interests and motives shift and evolve during the production process, the end result changes with him. Because, as he frequently confesses, he is very much ruled by his subconscious instincts, there are depths and recesses within his films which even he cannot consciously penetrate. If that is so, what chance do we have?

Furthermore, each new film casts a new light on all those which came before it. Therefore, there can be no such thing as A Grand Unified Theory of Gilliam, just an endless supply of subjects for debate.

You've read my contentions. I look forward to reading your ripostes in your own magazines or books, or even through the good orifice of *alt.movies.terry-gilliam*.

In some respects, Phil Stubbs has got the right idea with his excellent *Dreams* website. Because of the medium in which he publishes it, it remains open to change, constantly updateable, endless. The book you hold in your hand exists in this finished form only. Unless you fancy adding notes in the margins, the text won't change, the amount of information contained herein, won't fluctuate. It's done and dusted.

Yet, as I write, Gilliam is immersed in pre-production on his version of *Don Quixote*. Will he manage what Orson Welles never did? Will he actually get Cervantes' mighty tome up there on the screen? I dunno. But, if you come back to this book in two or three years time, you will.

Whatever the future of *this* book, *the* book on the work of Terry Gilliam, one of the few genuine artists working in the celluloid medium today, is very far from closed.

Of course, if *Don Quixote doesn't* make it to the big screen, it will be in distinguished company since Gilliam's track record in failing to get films made is almost as impressive as the list of his successes. Here are just a few of the films which may, or may not, be rescued from the back burner for eventual completion:

Gormenghast: The legendarily unfilmable book was 'in limbo' for decades before the BBC spectacularly sank their teeth into it. Gilliam's name was attached to various proposed film versions, stretching as far back as his days with Python. Hollywood logic being what it is, now that a perfectly good version exists there will doubtless be vast amounts of money thrown at an unnecessary big-screen rendition. Gilliam has stated that he is no longer interested.

Looney Tunes: This was a project about a man who turns into a cartoon. Since Gilliam dropped this idea, *Volere, Volare* (1991) and *The Mask* (1994) have taken it in radically different directions.

A Connecticut Yankee In King Arthur's Court: Gilliam was involved in bringing out the darker, more satirical side of Mark Twain's much abused classic in an attempt to bury the memory of Bing Crosby. 'Twas not to be.

The Hunchback Of Notre Dame: This was to be a vehicle for that French national monument Gerard Depardieu, based on a script by Rupert Walters, who wrote *Restoration* (1996). Work ground to a halt when Disney's masterful animated version appeared and essentially left very little for Gilliam to add.

The Hitchhiker's Guide To The Galaxy: Another project which has been around the block more times than a lost jogger. Given the obvious comparisons between Gilliam and Douglas Adams' track records, if anyone is going to make it, it really ought to be Gilliam.

Fungus The Bogeyman: This project came Gilliam's way in the backwash of *Munchausen*. They actually got as far as building a full-size Bogeyman suit, and there were plans to assemble as many of the usual Gilliam gang of collaborators and ex-Pythons as inclination and life expectancy would allow. Then they just stopped.

Watchmen: Undoubtedly the most well-known of Gilliam's unfilms. This was going to be a monstrous production, adapting Alan Moore and Dave Gibbon's hugely complex graphic novel about a world where superheroes are a lot less super than they appear. This film would have necessitated Gilliam being sucked into the uncontrollable maelstrom of the Hollywood mainstream. However, the money was not forthcoming. And besides, as Gilliam and Charles McKeown worked on the script, they became more and more distressed at the swathes of the book they were having to remove in order to fit it into a two-hour movie. Maybe it'll re-emerge one day, rather like *Gormenghast*, as a big-budget miniseries.

Time Bandits 2: Although Gilliam insists he wouldn't direct this, he and Charles McKeown worked out a detailed plot, involving all the surviving characters from the first film. Problem is, the story had The Supreme Being gearing up to destroy the Earth at the turn of the new Millennium. So, it would seem that time has beaten them. Either that, or we've got a *very* long wait.

A Scanner Darkly: Philip K Dick seems to be Hollywood's science fiction writer of choice, given that his works have formed the basis of *Blade Runner* (1982), *Total Recall* (1990) and Steven Spielberg's on-again, off-again production *Minority Report*. Nevertheless, this fact failed to secure funding for this adaptation, based on a script *The Fisher King*'s Richard LaGravenese and Gilliam were all fired up to write. Gilliam has reputedly not given up on this one.

A Tale Of Two Cities: Never too proud to let his friends remind him they told him so, Gilliam got involved in another big-budget, big-studio, big-star project. Then, in 1994, said big star Mel Gibson, decided he'd rather direct *Braveheart*. Liam Neeson (fresh from *Schindler's List*) stepped in, but the studio decided to cut the budget by more than half as a reflection of their lack of faith in Neeson. At that point Gilliam packed his bags and went back home.

Theseus And The Minotaur: This was originally planned, along with *Time Bandits* and *Brazil*, as a possible follow-up to *Jabberwocky*. A script was written by Gilliam and Bill Nicholsen, but no further progress was made. Then, in the mid-90s, Gilliam decided he was interested in the story again, and brought in Tony Grisoni (prior to working with him on *Fear And Loathing*) for a rewrite. They are reportedly still fiddling with this idea.

The Defective Detective: Co-written by Gilliam and Richard LaGravenese. This film, about a burnt out cop who falls into a child's fantasy world, was all ready to go in the glow of the success of *12 Monkeys*. Nicolas Cage (with his shiny new *Leaving Las Vegas* Oscar) had been cast. Storyboards were drawn. Everyone was raring to go. Gilliam swore that if the studio pulled out, he would turn his back on Hollywood forever. The studio pulled out.

Which brings us nicely to...

(The Man Who Killed) Don Quixote: Cervantes' tale about a deluded man who believes himself to be a medieval knight, is perfect Gilliam material. He and Charles McKeown have worked on the script on and off for about a decade. Then it was announced that Fred Schepisi was to make a version with John Cleese and Robin Williams. Gilliam, feeling betrayed, began to look around for another project, until he learned that the Schepisi project had sunk. *Quixote* is back on again, with a new script by Tony Grisoni. Johnny Depp is inked in to play Sancho Panza, with Jean Rochefort, Vanessa Paradis, Jonathan Pryce and Madeleine Stowe all pencilled in for various roles. Will this be the latest Gilliam unfilm? Time will certainly tell.

And now, as I endeavour to draw a veil over this volume, news is emerging of another contender for the unfilm files...

Good Omens: Long in limbo, Terry Pratchett and Neil Gaiman's sideways take on *The Omen* (1976) seems to have re-emerged from the Hollywood undergrowth, with Gilliam's name tentatively attached. When I interviewed Neil Gaiman about this book, many years ago, he explained that he and Terry Pratchett were greatly amused by Hollywood's attempts to package their novel. It seemed unlikely that it would make it to the big screen then. It seems no less unlikely now.

Resource Materials
Films By Gilliam

On Video

Monty Python And The Holy Grail, Fox Video, 2146C, £12.99
Jabberwocky, Fox Video, 4270S, Deleted
Time Bandits (Widescreen), CIC, VHR2781, £10.99
Monty Python's The Meaning Of Life, Polygram, 0447313, £10.99
Brazil (Widescreen), Warner Beyond Vision, SD36136, £12.99
The Adventures Of Baron Munchausen, Cinema Club, CC7144, Deleted
The Fisher King, Columbia Tri-Star, CVR22490, £10.99
12 Monkeys (Widescreen + *The Hamster Factor*), Polygram, 0519283, £9.99
Fear And Loathing In Las Vegas (Widescreen), CIC, 0618203, £15.99

On DVD

Given the ever-improving availability of multi-region DVD players, I have included the British Region 2 discs and the generally far superior American Region 1 disc.

Monty Python And The Holy Grail, (Widescreen) Region 1, Columbia/Tri-Star, 0767824571, $24.95

Time Bandits (Widescreen + Audio Commentary) Region 1, Criterion, 6305283699, $39.95

Brazil Box Set (Widescreen + Audio Commentary + Documentaries + Alternative Version) Region 1, Criterion, 0780022181, $59.95

The Adventures Of Baron Munchausen, (Widescreen) Region 2, Columbia/Tri-Star, CDR91774. £19.99

The Fisher King (Widescreen) Region 1, Columbia/Tri-Star, 0767811089, $27.95

12 Monkeys (Widescreen + *The Hamster Factor*) Region 2, Polygram, 0519202, £17.99

12 Monkeys (Widescreen + Audio Commentary + *The Hamster Factor*) Region 1, Universal, 078322608X, $34.98

Fear And Loathing In Las Vegas (Widescreen) Region 1, Universal, 0783229526, $26.98

Books By Gilliam

Harvey Kurtzman's Fun And Games by Charles Alverson, compiled by Harvey Kurtzman and Gilliam, Fawcett, 1965

The Cocktail People by Joel Siegel, cartoons by Gilliam, Pisani Press, 1966

Monty Python's Big Red Book, edited by Eric Idle, some illustrations by Gilliam, Eyre Methuen, 1972. Published in US by Warners in 1975

The Brand New Monty Python Book, edited by Eric Idle, illustrated by Peter Brookes and Jerry Gillian (no relation!) Eyre Methuen, 1973, published in the US as *The Brand New Monty Python Paperback*, 1974

Sporting Relations by Roger McGough, illustrations by Gilliam, Eyre Methuen, 1974

Monti Python ik den Holie Grailen (Bok), profusely illustrated by Gilliam. Eyre Methuen, 1977, published in the US as *Monty Python's Second Film: A First Draft*, Methuen, 1977

Jabberwocky: The Novel by Ralph Hoover, based on the script by Gilliam and Charles Alverson, Pan Books, 1977

Animations Of Mortality by Lucinda Cowell, profusely illustrated by Gilliam, Eyre Methuen, 1978

Monty Python's Life Of Brian / Montypythonscrapbook, edited by Eric Idle, illustrated by Gilliam, Grosset, 1979

The Complete Works Of Shakespeare And Monty Python: Vol One--Monty Python (containing *Monty Python's Big Red Book* and *The Brand New Monty Python Book*), Eyre Methuen, 1981

Time Bandits: The Script by Gilliam and Michael Palin, Dolphin Books, 1981

Time Bandits: The Novel by Charles Alverson, Sparrow Books, 1981

Monty Python's The Meaning Of Life, partly illustrated by Gilliam, Methuen, 1983

The Complete Monty Python's Flying Circus: All the Words, co-written by all the Pythons, Pantheon, 1989

The Adventures Of Baron Munchausen: The Screenplay by Gilliam and Charles McKeown, based on the novel by RE Raspe, Applause, 1989

The Adventures Of Baron Munchausen: The Novel by Gilliam and Charles McKeown, illustrated by James Victore and Joyce L Houlihan, Applause, 1989

The Fisher King: The Book Of The Film, Richard LaGravenese, with frequent interruptions from Gilliam, Applause, 1991

Fear And Loathing In Las Vegas - Not The Screenplay by Terry Gilliam and Tony Grisoni, based on the book by Hunter S Thompson, Applause, 1998

Brazil: The First Draft by Terry Gilliam and Charles Alverson, edited by Bob McCabe, Orion Books, 2000

Awards

Monty Python's Flying Circus

Special Award for Graphics, The British Academy of Film and Television Arts, 1969

Silver Rose, Montreux Television Festival, 1971

Monty Python's The Meaning Of Life

Grand Prix Special du Jury award, Cannes Film Festival, 1983

Brazil

Best Picture, Los Angeles Film Critics Association Awards, 1985
Best Director, Los Angeles Film Critics Association Awards, 1985
Best Screenplay, Los Angeles Film Critics Association Awards, 1985
Nominations:
Best Art/Set Direction, Academy Awards, 1985
Best Original Screenplay, Academy Awards, 1985

The Adventures Of Baron Munchausen

Nominations:
Best Art/Set Decoration, Academy Awards, 1989
Best Costume, Academy Awards, 1989
Best Make-up, Academy Awards, 1989
Best Special Effects, Academy Awards, 1989

The Fisher King

Best Supporting Actress (Ruehl), Academy Awards, 1991
Best Actor in a Musical/Comedy (Williams), Golden Globe Awards, 1992
Best Supporting Actress (Ruehl), Golden Globe Awards, 1992
Best Actress (Ruehl), Los Angeles Film Critics Association Awards, 1991
Nominations:
Best Actor (Williams), Academy Awards, 1991
Best Art/Set Decoration, Academy Awards, 1991
Best Original Screenplay, Academy Awards, 1991
Best Original Score, Academy Awards, 1991

12 Monkeys

Best Supporting Actor (Pitt), Golden Globe Awards, 1996
Nominations:
Best Supporting Actor (Pitt), Academy Awards, 1995
Best Costume Design, Academy Awards, 1995
Best Male Performance (Pitt), MTV Movie Awards, 1996

General

Michael Balcon BAFTA Award for Outstanding British Contribution to Cinema, 1987, for Monty Python
Honorary DFA, Occidental College, 1987

Honorary DFA, Royal College of Art, 1989

General Bibliography

Boss, Pete, *Vile Bodies And Bad Medicine*, *Screen*, Vol 27 No 1, Jan - Feb 1986

Britton, Lippe, Williams & Wood (ed.), *The American Nightmare*, *Festival Of Festivals*, 1979

Bundtzen, Lynda K, *Monstrous Mothers*, *Film Quarterly*, Vol XL No3, Spring 1987

Carroll, Noel, *Nightmare And The Horror Film*, *Film Quarterly*, Vol XXXIV No 3, Spring 1981

Contemporary Authors New Revision Series, Vol 35, Gale, 1991

Contemporary Authors, Vol 113, Gale, 1985

Cottingham, J, *Descartes*, Oxford University Press, 1986

Donald, James (ed.), *Fantasy & The Cinema*, BFI Publishing, 1989

Dyer, Richard, *Entertainment And Utopia*, *Movie*, No 24

Glass, Fred, *Laugh At Obstacles*, *Jump Cut*, No 29

Hutton, John, *Nightmares Old And New*, *Jump Cut*, No 32

Jackson, Rosemary, *Fantasy: The Literature Of Subversion*, Methuen, 1981

Johnson, Kim 'Howard', *The Real Fantasist*, *Starlog Platinum Edition*, Spring 1994: 63-68

Kariel, Henry S, *The Endgame Of Postmodernism*, *Futures*, Feb 1990

Laplanche, J P & Pontalis, J P, *Language Of Psychoanalysis*

Morgan, David, *The Mad Adventures Of Terry Gilliam*, *Sight And Sound*, Vol 57 No 4, Autumn 1988

Penley, Constance, *The Future Of An Illusion*, Routledge, 1989

Raspe, Rudolph Erich, *The Adventures Of Baron Munchausen*, 1985, Harrap

Rubenstein, Lenny, *Interview With Michael Palin*, *Cineaste*, Vol XIV No2

Sammon, Paul M and Shay, Don, *Cinefex*, No 38, May 1989

Seiter, Ellen, *Television Utopias*, *Jump Cut*, No 32

Swift, Jonathan, *Gulliver's Travels*, Blackie and Son Ltd, 1908

Monty Python

Brown, Geoff, *Review Of Holy Grail*, *Monthly Film Bulletin*, April 1975

DeSena, Tony, *An Interview With Graham Chapman And Terry Gilliam*, *Aquarian*, July 21-28, 1982

Gow, Gordon, *Review Of Holy Grail*, *Films and Filming*, May 1975

Grossberger, Lewis, *Monty Python*, *People*, August 2, 1982

Meehan, Thomas, *And Now For Something Completely Different*, *New York Times Magazine*, April 18, 1976

Rider, David, *Review Of And Now For Something Completely Different*, *Films And Filming*, Jan 1972

Rubenstein, Lenny, *Monty Python's Flying Circus*, *Cineaste*, Vol III No 1

Jabberwocky

Brown, Geoff, *Review, Monthly Film Bulletin*, April 1977

Linfert, Carl (text), *Library Of Great Painters: Hieronymous Bosch*, Thames and Hudson, 1972

Strechow, Wolfgang (text), *Library Of Great Painters: Pieter Bruegel*, Thames and Hudson, 1972

Stuart, Alexander, *Review, Films And Filming*, June 1977

Time Bandits

Photo-feature On Time Bandits, Starlog, No 55, Feb 1982

Dalton, Ruth, *Review, Film Directions*, No 16, 1982

Gaughn, Michael J, *Review, Film Quarterly*, Vol XXXVI No 1, Fall 1982

Gerrold, David, *Time Bandits And Scene Stealers, Starlog*, Jan 1982

Jones, Alan, *Review, Starburst*, Vol 4 No 1

Jones, Jerene, *The Only Yank In Monty Python Stares Down Critics As His Time Bandits Steals $24 Million, People*, Dec 21, 1981

Pym, John, *Review, Monthly Film Bulletin*, April 1981

Sulski, Jim, *Time Bandits: An Interview With Director, Writer And Producer Terry Gilliam, Fantastic Films,* April 1982

Thompson, Anne, *Bandit, Film Comment*, Vol XVII, Nov-Dec 1981

Brazil

Bennetts, Leslie, *How Terry Gilliam Found A Happy Ending For Brazil, New York Times*, 19/1/86

Glass, Fred, *Review, Film Quarterly*, Summer 1986

Johnson, Kim 'Howard', *Hello, Brazil, Starlog*, No 92, March 1985

Howell, Brian, *Interview With Terry Gilliam* and *Review, Films And Filming*, March 1985

Jones, Alan, *Review, Starburst*, Vol 7 No 7

Kinder, Marsha, *Back To The Future In The 80s..., Film Quarterly*, Vol XLII No 4, Spring 1989

Pirani, Adam, *The Many Faces Of Ian Holm, Starlog*, Oct 1985

Powers, John, *Review, LA Weekly*, Jan 17, 1986

Pym, John, *Review, Monthly Film Bulletin*, Aug 1985

Roddick, Nick, *Just Crazy About Brazil, Stills*, Feb 1985

Rubenstein, Lenny, *Review, Cineaste*, 1985

Rushdie, Salman, *The Location Of Brazil, American Film*, Sept 1985

Turan, Kenneth, *Review, California Magazine*, Dec 1985

The Adventures Of Baron Munchausen

Review, Gentlemen's Quarterly, March 1989

Canby, Vincent, *How A Notorious Liar Might Have Lived*, *New York Times*, March 10, 1989

Finch, Mark, *Review*, *Monthly Film Bulletin*, March 1989

Fleming, John, *Baron Munchausen*, *Starburst*, Vol 2 No 10

Hinton, Hal, *Review Of The Adventures Of Baron Munchausen*, *Washington Post*, Dec 7, 1989

Howe, Desson, *Red-Hot Baron*, *Washington Post*, March 24, 1989

Johnson, Kim 'Howard', *Interview With Eric Idle*, *Starlog*, No 142, May 1989

Johnson, Kim 'Howard', *Terry Gilliam's Marvellous Travels & Campaigns*, *Starlog*, No 141, April 1989

Johnson, Kim 'Howard', *True Facts About The World's Greatest Lies*, *Starlog*, March 1989

Jones, Alan, *Cinefantastique*, Vol 19 No 4, May 1989

Mathews, Jack, *Earth To Gilliam*, *American Film*, March 1989, pp34-39, 56-58

McDonnell, David, *Liner Notes*, *Starlog*, April 1989, pp74

Morgan, David, *The Mad Adventures Of Terry Gilliam*, *Sight And Sound*, Autumn 1988

Penman, Ian, *Monster Munch*, *The Face*, Vol 2 No 5, Feb 1989

Siskel, Gene, *Visual Overload*, *Chicago Tribune*, March 12, 1989

The Fisher King

Review Of The Fisher King, *New Republic*, Oct 21, 1991

Ansen, David, *The Holy Grail In The Unholy City*, *Newsweek*, Sep 23, 1991

Drucker, Elizabeth, *Review*, *American Film*, September/October 1991

Maslin, Janet, *A Cynic's Quest For Forgiveness*, *New York Times*, Sep 20, 1991

Panek, Richard, *A Writer's Dream*, *Premiere*, May 1991

Travers, Peter, *That Old Black Magic*, *Rolling Stone*, Oct 17, 1991

12 Monkeys

Review, *Chicago Sun-Times*, Jan 5, 1996

Dunn, Jancee, *Rebel Star*, *Rolling Stone*, April 3 1996

Gerston, Jill, *Terry Gilliam: Going Mainstream (Sort Of)*, *New York Times*, Dec 24, 1995

Gleiberman, Owen, *Number Of The Beasts*, *Entertainment Weekly*, Jan 12, 1996

Hutchinson, Tim, *Review*, *Film Review*, May 1996

James, Nick, *Time And The Machine*, *Sight And Sound*, April 1996

McCarthy, Todd, *Review*, *Premiere*, Feb 1996

Naughton, John, *Quiet! Genius At Work*, *Empire*, May 1996

Salisbury, Mark, *Review*, *Empire*, May 1996

Sloane, Judy, *Apocalypse Now*, *Film Review*, May 1996

Strick, Philip, *Review*, *Sight And Sound*, April 1996

Shulgasser, Barbara, *Grim, Gritty Story Of Fatal Virus*, *San Francisco Examiner*, Jan 5, 1996

Vincent, Mal, *Interview: Terry Gilliam On 12 Monkeys*, *Virginian-Pilot*, 1995, article reprinted on *Pilot Online*, Jan 1, 1996

Universal Pictures' *12 Monkeys Website Online Chat With Terry Gilliam*, Jan 4, 1996

Wilmington, Michael, *Worlds In Collision*, *Chicago Tribune*, Jan 14, 1996

Fear And Loathing In Las Vegas

Calcutt, Ian, *Review*, *Film Review*, Dec 1998

Hamilton, Jake, *Review*, *Empire*, Dec 1998

Leigh, Danny, *Listen I'm The Guy That Turned Down Forrest Gump*, *Neon*, Dec 1998

Smith, Adam, *Profile: Johnny Depp*, *Empire*, Dec 1998

Williams, Linda Ruth, *Review*, *Sight And Sound*, Nov 1998

Books About Python

Wilmut, Roger, *From Fringe To Flying Circus*, Methuen, 1980

Hewison, Robert, *Monty Python: The Case Against*, Methuen, 1981

Thompson, John O, (ed), *Monty Python: Complete And Utter Theory Of The Grotesque*, BFI Publishing, 1982

Perry, George, *Life Of Python*, Pavilion, 1983

Johnson, Kim 'Howard', *The First 200 Years Of Monty Python*, St. Martin's Press, 1989

Johnson, Kim 'Howard', *Life Before And After Monty Python*, Plexus, 1993

Morgan, David, *Monty Python Speaks!*, 4th Estate, 1999

Books About Gilliam

Yule, Andrew, *Losing The Light: Terry Gilliam And The Munchausen Saga*, Applause Books, 1991

Mathews, Jack, *The Battle Of Brazil*, Crown, 1987

Christie, Ian, *Gilliam On Gilliam*, Faber and Faber, 1999

McCabe, Bob, *Dark Knights And Holy Fools*, Orion, 1999

Websites About Gilliam

Dreams: The Terry Gilliam Fanzine: www.smart.co.uk/dreams/

This is the guv'nor of Gilliam sites; if you start here, you may never visit the others

The Terry Gilliam Files: members.aol.com/morgands1/closeup/indices/gillindx

Part of the site *WideAngle/Closeup*, run by journalist David Morgan, who has published many of the better Gilliam articles and interviews, a goodly number of which are archived here

Terry Gilliam's Brazil: www.trond.com/brazil/

If you really need to know that *Brazil* might well have been re-titled *The Ball Bearing Electro Memory Circuit Buster*, this is the website for you!

Brazil @ PythoNET: www.pythonet.org/brazil/

This is just one small part of the huge PythoNET site, which worships all the Pythons equally

The Adventures Of Baron Munchausen: www.mindspring.com/~coli/

12 Monkeys 'Things': www.geocities.com/Hollywood/Boulevard/8928/

And, lest we forget...

The Terry Gilliam News-Group is called alt.movies.terry-gilliam, and anyone can join in. I expect to see this book being roundly denounced on there, with your preferred theories being put forward instead. Don't let me down.

Contact the author: If you would like to correspond with John Ashbrook, and give him some feedback on this Pocket Essential, you can send an e-mail to: john.ashbrook@virgin.net

The Essential Library

If you've enjoyed this book why not try the following titles in the Pocket Essentials library?

New:
Terry Gilliam by John Ashbrook
Doctor Who by Mark Campbell

Published:
Woody Allen by Martin Fitzgerald
The Slayer Files: Buffy the Vampire Slayer by Peter Mann
Jackie Chan by Michelle Le Blanc & Colin Odell
The Brothers Coen by John Ashbrook & Ellen Cheshire
Film Noir by Paul Duncan
Heroic Bloodshed edited by Martin Fitzgerald
Alfred Hitchcock by Paul Duncan
Stanley Kubrick by Paul Duncan
David Lynch by Michelle Le Blanc & Colin Odell
Noir Fiction by Paul Duncan
Orson Welles by Martin Fitzgerald

Coming Up Soon:
Brian de Palma by John Ashbrook
The Simpsons by Peter Mann

Available at all good bookstores at £2.99 each, or order online at **www.pocketessentials.com**, or send a cheque to: **Pocket Essentials (Dept TG), 18 Coleswood Rd, Harpenden, Herts, AL5 1EQ, UK**
Please make cheques payable to 'Oldcastle Books.' Add 50p postage & packing for each book in the UK and £1 elsewhere.

US customers should contact Trafalgar Square Publishing, tel: 802-457-1911, fax: 802-457-1913, e-mail: tsquare@sover.net